# Hold 'em Poker
## for Advanced Players
### 21st Century Edition

*By*

David Sklansky AND Mason Malmuth

## A product of Two Plus Two Publishing

www.twoplustwo.com

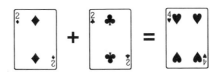

THIRD EDITION

SEVENTH PRINTING
October 2004

*Printing and Binding*
Creel Printing Co.
Las Vegas, Nevada

*Printed in the United States of America*

# Hold 'em Poker for Advanced Players

For information contact:   **Two Plus Two Publishing**
**600 West Sunset; Suite 103**
**Henderson, NV 89015**
**(702) 896-1326**
**www.twoplustwo.com**

ISBN: 1-880685-22-1

# Table of Contents

# Foreword
## by Ray Zee

Texas hold 'em is hard. There is probably no other form of poker as difficult. Yet, the game appears deceptively simple. Many players, even after much experience at the poker tables, still play as though any two cards can win. Of course, those who play in this fashion quickly lose their money.

The book you are holding, written by David Sklansky and Mason Malmuth, has had far-reaching effects on the poker world. Simply put, since the original edition of this book, hold 'em has become, on average, a much tougher game to beat.

If you have aspirations of being a serious player you will have to study the strategies and techniques in this text or you will be left behind. If you are new to the game, but are willing to put in the requisite time and effort, you soon will be more proficient at this form of poker than many of today's professional players. However, don't expect to become an expert overnight.

In *Hold 'em Poker For Advanced Players,* the authors provide not only numerous sophisticated concepts, but lots of examples as well. Many of these advanced strategies never appeared correctly in print until the first edition was originally released in 1988. With the twenty-first century edition, they have done it again. Much of the material that follows will be brand new to even successful professional players. Put another way, I stated in 1988 that "Numerous concepts contained in this book are well-understood only by a very small group of players — extremely successful players, I might add." Again, this statement is true today.

This brings up another point. This is one of the very few poker books actually written by winning players, and the authors thoroughly explain the techniques that have made them so successful at the tables. In addition, I know both authors quite well, and I know that no winning information was held back.

I have mixed feelings about seeing this book published, as I did when the original edition came out. As a professional poker player I'm not in favor of anything that will make the poker games tougher to beat. On the other hand, this new and expanded version of *Hold 'em Poker for Advanced Players* should help to spread this extremely interesting game just as the original edition did, and to make it even more popular. Thus there will be more games to choose from and there will still be plenty of good games. Consequently, I guess it is for the best that this twenty-first century edition is now available.

Finally, let me repeat that the techniques and ideas offered in this text should make any disciplined and studious player a significant winner. However, as already stated, it won't happen overnight. Most players will have to reread the book and study the concepts many times. In fact, I suspect that some of you will literally wear the covers off your copies of *Hold 'em Poker for Advanced Players*. But I know that those of you who do will be very happy with your results.

**Special note:** The authors would like to thank world class poker player Ray Zee for sharing many of his concepts and ideas with us. Because of Ray, this text is a better work.

# About David Sklansky

David Sklansky is generally considered the number one authority on gambling in the world today. Besides his nine books on the subject, David also has produced two videos and numerous writings for various gaming publications. His occasional poker seminars always receive an enthusiastic reception including those given at the Taj Mahal in Atlantic City and the World Series of Poker in Las Vegas.

More recently David has been doing consulting work for casinos, Internet gaming sites, and gaming device companies. He has recently invented a new game called *Poker Challenge,* soon to appear in casinos.

David attributes his standing in the gambling community to three things:

1.  The fact that he presents his ideas as simply as possible (sometimes with Mason Malmuth) even though these ideas frequently involve concepts that are deep, subtle, and not to be found elsewhere.
2.  The fact that the things he says and writes can be counted on to be accurate.
3.  The fact that to this day a large portion of his income is still derived from gambling (usually poker but occasionally blackjack, sports betting, horses, video games, casino promotions, or casino tournaments).

Thus, those who depend on David's advice know that he still depends on it himself.

### Other Books by David Sklansky

*Hold 'em Poker*
*The Theory of Poker*
*Getting The Best of It*

*Sklansky on Poker*
*Poker, Gaming, and Life*
*Sklansky Talks Blackjack*

*Gambling for a Living* by David Sklansky and Mason Malmuth
*Seven-Card Stud for Advanced Players* by David Sklansky, Mason Malmuth, and Ray Zee

# About Mason Malmuth

Mason Malmuth was born and raised in Coral Gables, Florida. In 1973 he received his BS in Mathematics from Virginia Tech, and completed their Masters' program in 1975. While working for the United States Census Bureau in 1978, Mason stopped overnight in Las Vegas while driving to his new assignment in California. He was immediately fascinated by the games, and gambling became his major interest.

After arriving in California he discovered that poker was legal and began playing in some of the public cardrooms as well as taking periodic trips to Las Vegas where he would play both poker and blackjack. In 1981 he went to work for the Northrop Corporation as a mathematician and moved to Los Angeles where he could conviently pursue his interest in poker in the large public cardrooms in Gardena, Bell Gardens, and Commerce.

In 1983 his first article "Card Domination — The Ultimate Blackjack Weapon" was published in *Gambling Times* magazine. In 1987 he left his job with the Northrop Corporation to begin a career as both a full-time gambler and a gambling writer. He has had over 500 articles published in various magazines and is the author or co-author of 12 books. These include *Gambling Theory and Other Topics,* where he tries to demonstrate why only a small number of people are highly successful at gambling. In this book he introduces the reader to the concept of "non-self weighting strategies" and explains why successful gambling is actually a balance of luck and skill. Other books he has co-authored are *Hold 'em Poker For Advanced Players,* written with David Sklansky, and *Seven-Card Stud For Advanced Players* written with David Sklansky and Ray Zee. All the "advanced" books are considered the definitive works on these games.

His company Two Plus Two Publishing has sold over 300,000 books and currently has 22 titles to its credit. These books are recognized as the best in their field and are thoroughly studied by those individuals who take gambling seriously.

### Other Books by Mason Malmth

*Gambling Theory and Other Topics*
*Poker Essays*
*Poker Essays, Volume II*
*Blackjack Essays*
*Winning Concepts in Draw and Lowball*

*Gambling for a Living* by David Sklansky and Mason Malmuth
*Seven-Card Stud for Advanced Players* by David Sklansky,
Mason Malmuth, and Ray Zee

### Booklets with Mason Malmuth

*Fundamentals of Craps* by Mason Malmuth and Lynne Loomis
*Fundamentals of Poker* by Mason Malmuth and Lynne Loomis
*Fundamentals of "21"* by Mason Malmuth and Lynne Loomis
*Fundamentals of Video Poker* by Mason Malmuth and Lynne
Loomis

# Introduction

Texas hold 'em is an extremely complicated form of poker. This is because the exact manner in which a hand should be played is often debatable. It is not uncommon to hear two expert players argue the pros and cons of a certain strategy. This means that even though you are about to read solid guidelines to winning, the strategies given are not set in concrete, and under certain conditions the best strategies may be different from those that are recommended.

On the other hand, the strategies in this text definitely provide a strong winning approach. If this were not the case neither author would be in a position to write this book, simply because we would both be broke and standing on the rail.

The "winning approach" we provide is a tight but aggressive one. It is not a "fast" approach, which some experts use to win slightly more money.[1] The reason for this is simply that most players who attempt to play fast will fail, as they do not have the judgment to handle the many situations that come up where they have put themselves in jeopardy. In any case, becoming an expert hold 'em player, even with the help of this book, will not be easy. It will require not only a great deal of study, but also a great deal of thinking, plus many hours of playing time at the hold 'em tables.

Keep in mind that the following strategies are designed for medium limit games, that is $10-$20 hold 'em up to (and including) $40-$80 hold 'em. In smaller games, or games that feature people who play too many hands and go too far with their

---

[1]Some experts deliberately play a few extra hands, and then use their superior playing skills to catch up. They still lose money on these additional hands, but these hands allow them to make a little more on their legitimate hands due to the additional deception that they create.

1

hands, many of the sophisticated plays used to manipulate standard opponents into making errors do not work. This is because many of these players are not *aware* enough to be tricked. Also, the structure of some smaller games is proportionately different. In spite of this, many ideas in the book will help you in smaller games while you work your way up to the bigger ones. In addition, the discussion on how to play in loose games will be crucial for your success. As for the bigger hold 'em games, where players are capable of thinking at many different levels, an understanding of the information in this book, combined with a great deal of experience and some hard thinking about the game, is the only way to guarantee success.

Before the first edition of *Hold 'em Poker for Advanced Players* was published in 1988, we debated for a long time before deciding to release the information it contained. We thought the strategies presented would make many of the games we played in much tougher, and we both derived much of our income from playing poker. However, after considering the avalanche of hold 'em books — most of which were inaccurate — that were reaching the market, we believed it was only right to go ahead and produce the text.

Incidentally, *Hold 'em Poker for Advanced Players* is not meant to replace *Hold 'em Poker* by David Sklansky. In fact, we still consider that book absolutely must reading for anyone interested in learning the game. However, we intend to discuss many areas of hold 'em which that text either only touches on or does not address, and we intend to discuss these areas at a level of significant sophistication.

Six years after the first edition of *Hold 'em Poker for Advanced Players* appeared we put out an expanded edition. To our amazement, poker — and hold 'em in particular — had exploded across the country. This meant that if you became proficient at Texas hold 'em, there would be many good games to play in and lots of places where these games can be found.

But the games had also changed from the time this text first appeared. Specifically, players who just played tight didn't seem to be as prevalent as they were in 1988. Moreover, there were now many more players who played very aggressively (perhaps overly so), and loose, action play became much more common. In fact, hold 'em pots frequently become quite large, with a great deal of money sometimes going into the center of the table before the flop. This was very different from the way we remember hold 'em when both of us first began to play it.

There were probably many reasons why this happened, but it was clear to us that this text had a lot to do with it. Many of the plays that we explained — and that we only rarely saw before — were now commonplace. On the other hand, with numerous new players at the hold 'em tables, many of whom came to "gamble," it was not surprising that the pace of the games had accelerated.

This change didn't really affect the strategies that *Hold 'em Poker for Advanced Players* provided, but it did affect when certain concepts came into play. Again, as we pointed out in 1988, there is no substitute for experience, and to ensure success, you should be doing a great deal of thinking about the game. So in 1994 we produced the second edition of this book. We gave more examples and offered more detailed explanations. But the basic concepts from the first edition remained the same.

It is now a new century, and we have decided to continue the process that we began in 1994. But we have taken it one step further, we are going to cover much new territory. Many of you have complained that while *Hold 'em Poker for Advanced Players* was the "advanced" text, it did not explain in enough detail how to play in loose, low limit games. This has now been thoroughly addressed and those of you who are familiar with the so called "low limit" texts will see that our approach is very different and much more profitable. In addition, some of you felt that the section on short-handed play was not complete; this has also been addressed. We have also added many new concepts into the "body" of the manual. And, as we have said many times before, if you study hard, get a proper amount of experience, and do a great deal of thinking about the game, you should be well on the road to success.

## 4 Introduction

Finally, we would like to express our appreciation to Irving Sklansky for editing this work. Thanks to him our ideas are now more clearly stated and thus should be more easily understood. In addition, we would like to also thank Charmaine Dadian for her typing, proof reading, and assistance in the overall production of this text.

# Using This Book

As stated in the introduction, this book will require you to do a great deal of thinking. It is recommended that the whole book be read first, then you can return to those sections that require more study. Also, if you are new to hold 'em you should memorize the hand rankings and how to play the first two cards. We see no better way to master this area of play. However, after you have gained the requisite experience, you will begin to see where it is appropriate to deviate from "correct" strategy and you will begin to think in terms of the actual hand itself rather than hand "groups." Almost all top players do this, although you should not get carried away. The text will supply plenty of discussion in this area.

We also recommend that you not jump right into a $40-$80 or higher limit game. Even though the strategies in this book will win their share at the $40-$80 limit, especially if your opposition is not too tough, it is still better to start lower and work your way up. In a game as complex as Texas hold 'em, there is no substitute for experience.

Keep in mind, when trying to master hold 'em, that at times many of the following concepts will seem to contradict each other. For example, some concepts might recommend that you bet your hand right out, while other concepts will advise you to go for a check-raise. One of the keys to successful hold 'em play is to balance these ideas, which will help you select the best strategy the vast majority of the time.

Finally, the game that we address (unless otherwise noted) is a structured-limit game. This game has two blinds, both to the dealer's left, with the first (small) blind being either one-half or two-thirds the size of the second (big) blind. All bets and raises before the flop and on the flop are equal to the size of the big blind, and all bets and raises on fourth street (known as the turn) and fifth street (known as the river) are double the size of the big blind. If you play in a game with a different structure, some of the ideas and concepts that this text discusses will not be totally accurate and adjustments must be made. However, the section titled "Non-standard Games" should help you in this area.

# Why Play Texas Hold 'em?

There are many forms of poker, and you can win money at virtually all of them if you develop the right set of skills. So why play Texas hold 'em? Why is this the game of the present and future? And why, of all poker games, is this complex form your best bet?

The answer is easy. By playing hold 'em, the expert player can win the most money with only a reasonable amount of risk.

You win money at poker because of two important factors. First, some of your opponents play badly, and in extreme cases, literally give their money away. This seems to happen frequently in Texas hold 'em since any two cards can win. However, random hands do not win often enough to show a profit, and when they do win, they frequently must be played cautiously, which also minimizes their profitability. In addition, hands that appear similar in strength to the non-skilled player are often quite different from each other. For example, holding just an ace does not make your hand very strong. Yet players who do not understand these basic ideas seem to flock to hold 'em games. (If you want to verify this statement, just look at the hold 'em explosion that took place in California when the game became legal in 1987.)

The second reason you can win money when playing hold 'em is that this form of poker offers numerous opportunities for the expert player to make expert plays that extract additional money from unsuspecting opponents. This is less true of most other forms of poker.

We mentioned earlier that the risk factor in hold 'em is reasonable. The correct way to assess risk in a poker game is through a statistical measure known as the standard deviation. We won't discuss the standard deviation in detail here (see *Gambling Theory and Other Topics* by Mason Malmuth), but will reiterate that it is a measure of the amount of short-term luck in a game.

7

Specifically, the poorer the relationship between the expectation (win rate) and the standard deviation the larger the fluctuations that you — the skilled player — can go through. Or, put another way, the worse you can run. Consequently, you usually should prefer a poker game where your bankroll requirements when compared to the size of the game, are not too steep.

There is no question that once you have achieved expert status, hold 'em offers an excellent relationship between the expectation and the standard deviation. The reasons for this are that the best hand holds up more often in hold 'em than in any other game, and that you have the advantage of being able to see your opponent's last card which is yours as well. This means that sometimes you can throw away a hand that you would have to call with in other forms of poker, or you might be able to get in an extra bet, whereas in other games you might be forced to check.

Of course, hold 'em can still be very frustrating — especially when it seems as though your opponents are always making their two- or three-out hands. However, with the tremendous growth of hold 'em, along with what we have just stated, there is no question that anyone who becomes an expert at this game will do very well indeed.

# A Note on the English

Neither one of us claim to be professional writers. We are professional poker players. Furthermore, the ideas and concepts presented in this book originally came from tape recorded conversations between the authors. These tape recordings were not necessarily formatted exactly the same way a book would be and the language was not always grammatically perfect. This is occasionally reflected in the wording of this text.

But the purpose of this book is not to get an "A" from our English teacher. Rather it is to show you how to make a lot of money in all but the toughest hold 'em games. So if we end a sentence with a preposition or use a few too many words or even introduce a new subject in a slightly inappropriate place, you can take solace from the fact that you can buy lots more books by Hemingway with the money we make you.

# Part One
# The First Two Cards

# The First Two Cards

# Introduction

The one area of hold 'em play where many strict guidelines can be given is on the first two cards. This is because the number of possible combinations is not that great. However, this does not mean that every hand should be played the same way every time, or that playing the first two cards is easy. You occasionally should play a hand differently not only for the sake of variation, but also depending on whether the game is loose or tight, or passive or aggressive. Expert players must be fooled more often than poor ones. But even if poor players always have a good idea of exactly where you are, you will lose some of your edge.

Also, how loose and passive the game is can make a significant difference. Some hands that are not usually profitable to play become significant money winners if your opponents are non-aggressive. The opposite is also true. Hands that are normally worth a play should be discarded if a couple of very aggressive players are in the game, particularly if these players know what they are doing.

In addition, how well you play is very important. As your judgment improves, you should be able to play a few more hands than these guidelines suggest. But don't go overboard with this concept. Always remember tight, aggressive play will get the money. This is true no matter what you may observe in the short run. Sometimes you will see bad players taking down pot after pot. In the short run their play can look terrific, but in the long run this type of play does not get the money.

And finally, before we get started, keep in mind that hold 'em is a game that can easily cause you to go "on tilt." For instance, a hand like

can be very tempting to play, even from an early position, especially if you are losing.

A unique aspect of hold 'em is that hands you *don't* play can sometimes be frustrating because the board is always the same whether you play or not. There will be occasions when you would have made a strong hand had you not thrown away your cards. Do not let this affect you. Even though any two cards can win, random holdings don't win often enough to be profitable.

# Hand Rankings

To simplify the presentation of some of the strategies that follow, the starting hands have been placed in appropriate groupings. The reason for this is that most of the hands in each grouping can be played roughly the same before the flop in many, but not all, situations. However, there are many exceptions, which will be discussed in the text. In fact, the starting hands actually move up and down the hand rankings depending on the circumstance. Because of this, it can be a mistake to rigidly adhere to the hand rankings. Again, make sure that you understand all the discussion concerning how the individual hands play.

These hand rankings (with some modifications) first appeared in David Sklansky's book *Essays on Poker*.[2] They are slightly different from the rankings that appear in the original version (pre 1997) of Sklansky's book *Hold 'em Poker*. The alterations reflect the structure change from one small blind to two blinds which causes more multiway pots and higher pot odds — especially on the flop. Also reflected is the fact that the players have become tougher and generally more aggressive as the years have gone by.

This has raised the value of suited hands, especially suited connectors. Medium pairs also have gone up in value because you no longer should automatically give up when an overcard flops, especially if the pot is being contested short-handed.

The rankings are as follows, with an "s" indicating suited and an "x" indicating a small card. Note that a 10 is represented as "T." Also, if no "s" appears, then the hand is not suited. (These notations will be used throughout this book.)

**Group 1:** AA, KK, QQ, JJ, AKs

---

[2]*Essays on Poker* is today published as part of *Sklansky on Poker*.

**Group 2:** TT, AQs, AJs, KQs, AK

**Group 3:** 99, JTs, QJs, KJs, ATs, AQ

**Group 4:** T9s, KQ, 88, QTs, 98s, J9s, AJ, KTs

**Group 5:** 77, 87s, Q9s, T8s, KJ, QJ, JT, 76s, 97s, Axs, 65s

**Group 6:** 66, AT, 55, 86s, KT, QT, 54s, K9s, J8s, 75s

**Group 7:** 44, J9, 64s, T9, 53s, 33, 98, 43s, 22, Kxs, T7s, Q8s

**Group 8:** 87, A9, Q9, 76, 42s, 32s, 96s, 85s, J8, J7s, 65, 54, 74s, K9, T8

These rankings reflect not only which group each starting hand belongs to, but its approximate order in that group as well. In reality, it's usually only necessary to know in which group a starting hand belongs. Consequently, Tables I and II provide an easier scheme for memorizing the group for each starting hand. Any hand not listed in the tables is ranked below Group 8.

## Table I: Hand Groupings for Pairs

| Hand | Group | Hand | Group |
|------|-------|------|-------|
| AA | 1 | 77 | 5 |
| KK | 1 | 66 | 6 |
| QQ | 1 | 55 | 6 |
| JJ | 1 | 44 | 7 |
| TT | 2 | 33 | 7 |
| 99 | 3 | 22 | 7 |
| 88 | 4 | | |

## Table II: Hand Groupings For Non-Pairs

| Hand | Group | | Hand | Group | |
|---|---|---|---|---|---|
| | Suited | Not Suited | | Suited | Not Suited |
| AK | 1 | 2 | 98 | 4 | 7 |
| AQ | 2 | 3 | 97 | 5 | - |
| AJ | 2 | 4 | 96 | 8 | - |
| AT | 3 | 6 | | | |
| A9 | 5 | 8 | 87 | 5 | 8 |
| Ax | 5 | - | 86 | 6 | - |
| | | | 85 | 8 | - |
| KQ | 2 | 4 | | | |
| KJ | 3 | 5 | 76 | 5 | 8 |
| KT | 4 | 6 | 75 | 6 | - |
| K9 | 6 | 8 | 74 | 8 | - |
| Kx | 7 | - | | | |
| | | | 65 | 5 | 8 |
| QJ | 3 | 5 | 64 | 7 | - |
| QT | 4 | 6 | | | |
| Q9 | 5 | 8 | 54 | 6 | 8 |
| Q8 | 7 | - | 53 | 7 | - |
| | | | | | |
| JT | 3 | 5 | 43 | 7 | - |
| J9 | 4 | 7 | 42 | 8 | - |
| J8 | 6 | 8 | | | |
| J7 | 8 | - | 32 | 8 | - |
| | | | | | |
| T9 | 4 | 7 | | | |
| T8 | 5 | 8 | | | |
| T7 | 7 | - | | | |

If you are new to hold 'em we feel that it is very important to memorize these groupings. There is no way around this, and the tables make the task much easier. Once the tables are memorized, this system will facilitate applying many of the concepts that follow. (For those of you who are interested in the rationale behind these rankings, see *Hold 'em Poker* by David Sklansky.)

However, we want to state that by the time you reach expert status you shouldn't be thinking in terms of hand groups. At this point in your playing career your starting hand decisions should be based on the intrinsic value of each hand in each particular situation. But if you are just getting started playing, we know of no better approach.

# The First Two Cards: Early Position

Hold 'em is a positional game, perhaps more so than any other form of poker. This is because the button determines the order in which players act for all betting rounds. (The only exception to this are the blinds, who act last on the first betting round, but act first on all succeeding betting rounds.) Consequently, the number of hands that can be safely played from an early position — which we will define as the first three positions to the left of the big blind in a ten-handed game — is quite limited. Since you are out of position on all betting rounds, you need a superior starting hand to make it worth playing.[3]

Specifically, in early position in a typical hold 'em game, if you are the first one in, or if there is only a call to your right, be prepared to play only those hands in the first four groups. In a loose game, as long as the players are not too aggressive, you can add the Group 5 hands, especially the suited connectors. In a tough game, it is probably best to discard even the Group 4 hands. These guidelines are very important. Playing too many hands up front is one of the most costly errors that you can make.

Even though we just said that you can play the Group 5 hands in non-aggressive loose games, notice that we said "especially the suited connectors." The game would have to be almost perfect for hands like

---

[3]A fuller treatment of the importance of position can be found in both *Hold 'em Poker* and *The Theory of Poker* by David Sklansky.

or

to be playable in an early position.

Furthermore, as the game gets more aggressive, you should discard some of the weaker Group 4 hands such as AJ and KTs. These can be difficult hands to play out of position, especially if you find yourself isolated by an aggressive player.

When we refer to a game as *loose,* we mean a game without much before-the-flop raising and with many players in most pots. (This game would actually be loose and passive.) When we say *tough*, we mean a game with a fair amount of raising, but not many large multiway pots. (This game would actually be tight and aggressive.) There's also a type of game where several players play very well, but only once the flop comes. If you are not sure which of these types you are playing, it is best to assume that the game is typical until you can determine otherwise. Remember that big pots do not necessarily make a game good. If the big pots are created by a lot of tactically sound raising, your best strategy might be to look for a softer game.

We also want to point out that loose and passive are not the same thing. If a game is loose, but still very aggressive, you should not be in many pots. On the other hand, you could play a fair number of hands in a tight but passive game.

Put another way, passive/aggressive should have a major impact on the number of hands that you play, while loose/tight should impact the mix of hands that you play. There will be more discussion of this throughout the text.

Sometimes you will need to add a few hands to those you play up front to throw your opponents off. For example, you occasionally should play a hand like

in an early position, even if the game is tough, to stop your more observant opponents from stealing against you when "rags" flop. Also, this is a good hand to occasionally raise with if you feel that your early position raises are getting too much respect. (That is you are not getting any action.) However, no matter what the reason for playing a hand like this, make sure that your hand is suited, and only do this occasionally.

If there is a raise to your right and the game is typical or tough, you should limit your play to those hands in Groups 1 and 2. Against an extremely tight player in a tough game, it may be correct to throw away some of the Group 2 hands, such as:

and

(Remember that this chapter refers to early-position decisions.)

If there is a raise to your right and the game is loose, you should be able to safely play Group 3 hands as well. However, beware of AQ. Even in a loose game, this hand does not play well against an early-position raiser if many players remain to act behind you. (Of course, if the AQ is suited, you definitely would play the hand.)

We want to pause and point out that you should not be calling many raises if no one else (except the raiser) has voluntarily entered the pot when playing hold 'em, no matter what your position or what your two starting cards are. You should usually either fold or occasionally reraise. We just mentioned that if the game is loose it can be correct to play a Group 3 hand in a raised pot. However, to call a raise with a hand like

before anyone else is in you need to be very sure that several other players are coming. If you are consistently wrong it can prove to be quite costly to your overall strategy. (The exception is if you are in the blind. This will be addressed later in the text.)

While we are on the subject we also want to address loose raisers. That is players who have weak raising standards and thus frequently are first to put two bets in the pot. If you follow the above guidelines, you will mainly be playing only Group 1 and 2 hands against an early position raiser. However, against the aforementioned loose raiser you should go ahead and play AQ, 99, and 88, and probably reraise with them. (You should also be reraising with the Group 1 and Group 2 hands with the exception of AJs and KQs which are still best to just call with.) Again, for this play to be correct your judgment must be accurate. If you are not sure it is probably best to throw these additional hands away. (Also note that we are making a distinction between a loose raiser and a loose game.)

If no one has yet called, almost always raise with AA, KK, QQ, AK, and AQ. Part of the reason to raise with these hands is that they lose value as the pot gets more multiway (especially if your opponents see the flop for one bet rather than two). If there have already been callers, usually raise with hands in Groups 1 and 2, AQ, and perhaps some other hands at random. (Again, these random raises should be made only occasionally.)

Also, if no one has voluntarily put money in the pot, you should raise approximately two-thirds of the time with AKs, AQs, AJs, and KQs. The reason for sometimes calling with these hands is not only for deception purposes, but also because they play well in multiway pots. However, because of the large blind structure in today's game, it is not necessary to just call with these hands very often. In fact, against weak opposition, it is best to almost always raise with them, since the deception you are trying to gain by just calling won't do you much good anyway. On the other hand, if the game is tight and most players respect your raise, be more inclined to limp with the big suited connectors. Again, these hands play well in multiway pots.

You may also occasionally limp with AA or KK. The time to do this would be when your early position raises are not getting any callers. If raised, you would frequently, but not always reraise. (However, if you are heads-up and are raised we suggest that you usually just call with aces or kings to add deception against your one opponent. Then plan to raise on fourth street.) In addition, be less inclined to limp with two kings as opposed to two aces. This is because with a pair of kings, an overcard — the ace — can come on the flop, while no overcards can come to a pair of aces.

Finally, if no one has yet called, raise approximately one-third of the time with a hand like

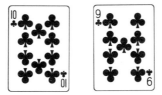

as long as the game is typical or tough. This is mainly for deception purposes. Again, keep in mind how strong your competition is. If you are in a game full of extremely weak opponents, it is generally best to simply call with these hands. That is, in a game where most of your opponents are going to come anyway, this play will lose its value.

By the way, if you call with a large suited connector and are raised, go ahead and reraise with AKs and possibly with AQs. In addition, if a lot of people are in the pot, you sometimes can reraise with a hand like:

The reason for this last raise requires some explanation and will be better understood after you get further into the book. Basically, you are making the pot larger so that if you get a flop you like, such as two flush cards of the appropriate suit, then more of your opponents will be encouraged to stay for one or two more cards with as little as one overcard.

Let's return to loose games. Keep in mind that some hands, such as

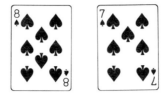

play well against many opponents. If there are usually a lot of callers but not much raising, these types of hands become playable in early position. However, overplaying these hands up front — and most players do just that — can get you into trouble. Make sure that the requirement of loose and passive is met. Again, if you are not sure, it is usually best to pass on these hands in an early position.

The same is true of small pairs such as:

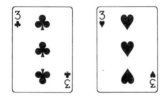

They can be played from an early position providing that you are sure that you will get a multiway pot. However, they can stand a little more action than the suited connectors. But if many pots are going to three bets or more, they are probably never worth playing, even if you can usually anticipate several opponents.

One criteria to keep in mind when deciding to play a small pair or a medium to small suited connector is how passive/aggressive the game is, in addition to its being loose. Specifically, as just mentioned, small pairs play well in loose aggressive games providing that they are not too aggressive. This is because if you flop a set you can anticipate many bets going into the pot. If the game is too aggressive and you hold a small pair you will frequently be forced to play for several bets, and now your hand will not achieve the implied odds that it needs to be profitable.

If the game is passive, you prefer the suited connector to the small pair. This is because a "set" will have trouble collecting a lot of bets. On the other hand, if the suited connector flops something like a gut shot draw it won't necessarily be bet out of the pot.

Here's an example of this last idea. Suppose you start with the 8♠7♠ mentioned above and the flop comes:

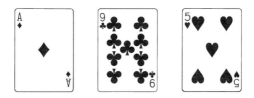

If the game is passive you may still be around on fourth or fifth street to catch a six if it slides off. If the game is aggressive you may find yourself out of the hand.

Sometimes the game will be moderately aggressive but will feature two or three players who will play virtually any ace. In games like this, (and they are very common even at limits as high as $20-$40), we recommend that you play A9s, A8s, 77, and 66 as long as the pot is not yet raised. Now if you hit your ace someone may have aces with you, but with a worse kicker, or if you flop your set someone may call a bet trying to catch that elusive ace.

One hand that we have not yet addressed is a pair of jacks in the pocket. If no one has opened and you are in an early position, it is usually best to raise with JJ in a tight game and to just call with it in a loose game. With two jacks you would prefer either to have no more than one or two opponents in the hope that your hand holds up without improvement, or to have as many opponents as possible when the majority of your profits come from flopping three-of-a-kind. The worst scenario is when *exactly* three or four opponents see the flop with you. This most likely would occur if you called in a tight game or raised in a loose game.

If you hold JJ and the pot has been raised and reraised before the action gets to you, you should fold. This is correct even when you are in a middle or late position. However, if you have already opened with JJ and the pot has been raised and reraised behind you, then it is correct to go ahead and call because of the pot odds. What you are hoping to do in this situation is to flop trips. If you do not make a set, be prepared to fold (although folding is not necessarily automatic).

# The First Two Cards: Middle Position

Playing your hand from a middle position, which we will define as the fourth, fifth, and sixth positions to the left of the big blind, is similar to the play of your hands from an early position. The main difference is that you now can play a few more hands, since your positional disadvantage is not as great.

This means that in an unraised pot, you can play all hands in Groups 1-5 when the game is typical or tough. In a loose, passive game it is all right to play the Group 6 hands as well.

However, if the game is loose, aggressive, some of the weaker hands such as

and

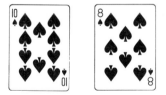

should probably be thrown away. You will find it difficult to "steal the blinds" as someone in a later position may be quick to try to isolate you (make it three bets) if you come in with a raise.

Also, if you are not the first one in, consider the strength of your opponents. Specifically, the weaker your opponents are, the more hands you can play. Put another way, you should be more inclined to play marginal hands only against poorer players.

Small pairs and medium suited connectors should also be played differently than you would play them in early position if you are first in, and the game is loose. Up front, you should enter the pot if the game conditions are right. But if you are in middle position and no one has voluntarily entered the pot means that it is unlikely that you will get the multiway action that these hands require.

Here's an example. Suppose the game is loose but not overly aggressive, and you expect pretty good action on most flops. It would now be correct to play

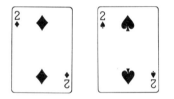

if you are first in from an early position. However, if the first three or four people pass in this exact same game, you should throw this hand away. (Note that we consider these players to have passed if they are away from the table as well as if they threw their hand away.) If you do play, in addition to not getting the multiway action that you wish, you may find yourself isolated by an aggressive player. Now unless you flop a set you will be playing a weak hand out of position. Similar comments apply for a hand like:

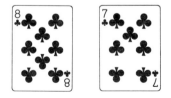

The situation changes if there are already one or more players in and you can anticipate a multiway pot. Now the 2♦2♠ or the 8♣7♣ may become playable if the game conditions are right. (Remember, small pairs like games where there is a lot of action on the flop, while the connecting hands prefer more passive play.)

Another difference between early and middle position is that in middle position you virtually never just call as the first one in with the large suited connectors, such as:

One of the reasons for this is that some of your opponents will begin to suspect you of trying to steal the blinds (with weak hands) when you raise after several people have passed. So you may as well raise all of those times when you hold a good hand.

Thus, if you are the first one in, raise with all hands that are in Groups 1, 2, and 3. This is also usually correct if there have been callers to your right. However, when there are callers, don't always raise with the Group 3 hands. If you hold a Group 3 hand, consider how well your opponents play and whether you want a lot of players or a few players. If your opponents are strong, tend to call; otherwise, raise. When you want a lot of opponents, such as with JTs as opposed to AQ, this is another time to just call (when you are not the first one in) with a Group 3 hand.

It may also be correct to raise with Group 4 hands AJ or KQ. The time to do so is *when you think it is likely that your raise will*:
1.    Knock out most (if not all) of the players behind you.
2.    Keep the pot short-handed.

And no strong player has voluntarily entered the pot.

It also helps to have tight players in the blinds. If this is not the case, it is probably best to only call with these hands. And if someone has limped in who is likely to hold a dangerous hand such as AA or AKs — you should consider folding.

If the pot already has been raised, almost always reraise with AA, KK, QQ, AKs, and AK. In addition, occasionally reraise with other good hands, such as:

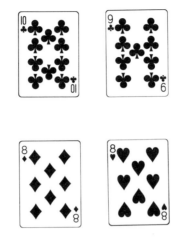

or

Remember, these raises are made so you can vary your play and throw some of your opponents off. Raising too often with these types of hands could prove to be very expensive. Moreover, you usually should throw these hands away if the pot already has been raised.

If the raiser is a "loose raiser" you should use the same guidelines as given for early position play when considering reraising with a hand like:

But remember, if you are not sure as to the correct course of action, it is probably best to throw the hand away.

One strategy that begins to come into play in the middle positions is that you *should almost always raise rather than call when:*

1.  No one has yet entered the pot.
2.  You have a playable hand (generally Group 1-6).
3.  You think there is a reasonable chance (perhaps as small as 25 percent), that all players behind you (including the blinds) will fold.

However, if criterion one or three is not met you should usually just call except with your best hands, and actually *fold* some of the weaker hands (basically Group 6) that you would have otherwise raised with.

# The First Two Cards: Late Position

On the button, and in the position just to the button's right (and sometimes in the position two to the button's right), much of what is correct play is quite different from what we have seen in the early and middle positions. One of the reasons for this is that you will have excellent position on all betting rounds which will enable you to make better decisions than you can make in the earlier positions. This is because when your opponents check or bet, you have gained a great deal of *information* about their hands, while they do not have this same information about your hand.

This means that in general you should tend to play aggressively if the pot is short-handed, unless the blinds and the remaining players are loose. If the pot is already multiway, however, you should be less aggressive unless you hold a hand that plays well in multiway pots.

You should understand that if you are in late position and are the first player to enter the pot, any hand that you should play is almost always worth a raise. This usually means hands in Groups 1-7, maybe those in Group 8, and even worse hands if you think your opponents are tight enough that you have a decent chance to steal the blinds. However, if there are already callers, only normally raise with hands in Groups 1-3, and sometimes with Group 4 hands (except if there are many players, do not raise with unsuited high cards, but conversely be somewhat inclined to raise with hands as weak as Group 5 if they are straight flush combinations).

For example, if you hold

and a lot of players are in the pot, it is probably best to just call (if there has not yet been a raise). On the other hand, if you have

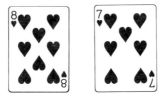

several players are already in the pot, and no one has yet raised, then raising is probably a good play.

But we should point out that you need to consider your opponents before raising with a hand like 8♥7♥. If you are against players who not only play too many hands, but go too far with their hands regardless of the size of the pot, there is less value to raising. Part of the reason for making this raise is to entice your opponents to continue on if you happen to get a flop to your liking. But if you are fairly sure that they will do precisely that anyway, then you should usually just call.

Another reason to raise is if you think it may "buy you the button." Being able to act last on succeeding betting rounds is a major advantage. Thus with marginal hands it may be worth raising if you think it will take that raise to get the button to fold.

Sometimes you can raise with some weaker hands in late position. This opportunity arises when you are against one or two callers who play poorly and did not enter the pot from the early positions (and thus probably have weak hands). If you have a playable hand that would prefer to play against a small number of opponents, and you believe that your raise will fold everyone out behind you, then you should raise. This would include hands like

A7s, KJ, QJ, and even a hand as weak as QT. However, if you don't think that everyone behind you will fold, you should not make this play and even consider folding some of these hands (e.g. QJ and QT).

One of the reasons for this type of raise is that against weak opposition (and, as usual, you always should consider your opponents when making your playing decisions), it allows you to "take control" of the pot. That is, if your opponents do not flop a hand, and you bet after they have checked, you often will be able to pick up the pot. This is especially true if a high card has flopped. In addition, if you choose not to bet on the flop, your raise may have gained you a free card. (More on this later in the text.)

Here's an example of this idea. Suppose you raise a weak player who calls from a middle position, and you hold:

If the flop comes something like

your opponent will likely check and fold, assuming that he does not flop anything, since he now will fear that you have a king.

You can also occasionally make this same play with a small pair or a suited connector such as:

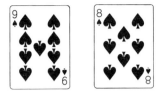

The time to do it would be when you have very good control over your opponent, you are very sure that everyone behind you will fold, and the blinds are tight. (Note: This will not usually be the case in many of today's games.)

Finally, when deciding if it is correct to make this type of play you need to have a good idea of what your opponent thinks of you. If your play scares him, be more inclined to go ahead with this type of raise. But keep in mind that these are volatile strategies that can backfire, especially if you have misjudged your opponent.

To call a raise *cold* you still need a very good hand, even in late position. However, if several people are already in the pot, even though it has been raised, you also can play hands like:

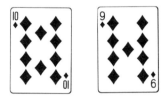

and

You can even play smaller pairs in this spot if you can anticipate at least five players. Even without this many you can still call the raise if you are against players who have the potential to lose many bets. If these conditions are met, it becomes correct to call with all pairs down through deuces.

If the raise is from a middle position or later you can play a few more hands if the raiser is the first one in and does not play well. (Being first in means that he is more likely to be raising with a weak hand because he may be trying to steal the blinds.) However, you still need to be cautious and never play a hand like:

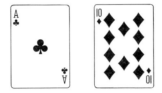

In addition, almost always reraise with any Group 1 hand, and as before, be prepared to reraise with hands as weak as AQ, 99, or 88 if it is a "loose raiser."

If the pot is not multiway and you are against a legitimate raise you can occasionally make it three bets with a medium pair or a hand like JTs. You don't need to be in a late position to make this play, but it is probably a little better if you are. A play like this is occasionally correct because if you only make it three bets with AK or a big pair you are giving away too much information. However, if you are against players who are not observant, and tend to automatically go too far with their hands, then this play would never be correct.

There is also a time when you would almost always reraise with weaker hands, even those as weak as Group 4. This occurs when your opponent is the first one in from a late position and he enters the pot with a raise. Notice that your opponent may be trying to steal the blinds, so a reraise on your part, with reasonably strong hands, becomes correct. However, with the exception of AJ and KQ, reraise with a Group 4 hand only if your opponent is a weak player and you believe you have excellent control over him. Otherwise, you are probably better off to limit yourself to Groups 1-3. If neither you nor your opponent flops a hand, your reraise not only may stop him from trying to steal the pot, but also may allow *you* to do the stealing. So again, the correct play on your part is to either reraise or fold before the flop. It is almost never correct to just call.

The above play can also be correct with pairs down through sixes and occasionally as weak as fours. However, for this to be the case, you need to be against someone who will quickly release on the flop or someone who will check it down if they have any doubt over their hand. This usually means a solid player who is winning in the game (and thus is not steaming), or an extremely weak player.

If you hold a hand like KT, QT, or JT, (all offsuit) and a couple of players have called from early or middle position, you should often throw it away. This would be particularly true if one of the limpers plays well. It will now be easy for you to hit your hand but still lose because you have made a second best hand. You should also discard any of these if one of the limpers, particularly the first player in, is known to limp with very good hands. However, against bad players who will come with many hands they are definitely playable.

If you are dead last — that is, if you are on the button — and there are already callers, you can play hands in Groups 1-7. If you have a small pair and are against four or more callers, the correct play is to sometimes raise. This is another example of making the pot larger so that if you hit your hand, your opponents may be more inclined to call you with just overcards on the flop. In addition, they all may check to you, thus giving you a free card and another (small) chance to make your set. Also, this play is sometimes correct with small suited connectors. Again, don't get carried away with these plays. But making them occasionally can be very effective.

If you are on the button, a lot of players are already in, and the pot is not raised, you can call with many additional hands. This includes those hands in Group 8 and even hands as weak as:

The reason for this is the tremendous implied odds that you will be getting if the flop comes just as you would like it to come. However, don't take this idea too far. It is unlikely that it would ever be correct to call with a hand like:

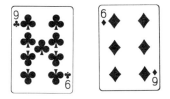

As already mentioned, if no one has called, you can raise the blinds from the last position (button) with any hand in Groups 1-8. With a hand like an ace with an unsuited weak kicker, you still should raise the blinds if they are either very tight or very weak players. When we say weak, we are referring to a player who will let your ace win in a showdown. For example, suppose you raise with something like

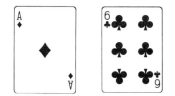

and are called by the blind. If this person is willing to check on the river with nothing, even if you show weakness by not betting on the turn, then he is the type of player you would be happy to play a lone ace against.

The same caveat applies to a hand like Kx, but even more so. That is, against typical opposition, usually pass with Kx. However, if you do play a hand like Kx on the button, make sure that you always raise. Never just call the blind if you are the first one in. (There is an exception to always raising with Ax or Kx if you play them first in on the button. See "Part Five: Playing Short-Handed" — "When the Blinds are Very Loose" on page 197)

# The First Two Cards: Live Blinds

Playing your first two cards out of the blinds is very different from the other positions because you will have terrible position for the next three rounds. But this is somewhat compensated for by the fact that you have to call only a partial bet. The net result is that you play rather tight in some situations, but quite loose in others.

Over their careers, many players lose quite a bit of money from the blind positions. This is because they frequently overestimate the value of their hand in comparison to the partial bet that they are required to make to continue playing. Even though you can play looser in some situations, you still must play fairly tight if the pot has been raised and the raiser is not in a steal position. More on this later.

First let us discuss the situation where you are in the (live) big blind and no one else has raised. In this case, you should usually raise only with extremely good hands. Remember, one of the reasons to raise in late position is to help you to take control of the pot. However, this is much harder to do when you are first to act on the flop.

Let's suppose you have

and one or two aggressive players have called from an early position. Your best play usually (but not always) is to just call and (perhaps) to try for a check-raise later. You don't have to hit your hand to make check-raising the correct play. You just need to be fairly sure that the flop did not help anyone else. An example might be a flop like:

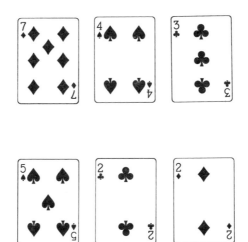

or

Since these were early-position players, there is an excellent chance that you have the best hand. You can check -raise if you think someone with a hand that is worse than your AK will bet in this spot.

However, if you hold AK in the big blind and are called by only one or two players from *late* positions, then you usually should raise. Because of their positions — and implied weakness when they just call — you cannot rule out any flop from hitting them. However, a raise is now the best play, since it is likely that your hand is far superior.

It also is sometimes correct to raise in the big blind when several people have called and you hold a hand like JTs, A5s, or a small pair. Keep in mind that this play is not as strong from the blind position as it is in late position because you will be unlikely to get a free card if you check. However, if the flop does come as you would like, your raise may entice some players to stay with hands that they *should* fold if they knew what you held. (See *The Theory of Poker* by David Sklansky for more discussion of this idea.)

Suppose you are the big blind, the pot has been called on your left, and someone now raises on your right. In this case, you should call only with your better hands. This is because you can be reraised on your left. Still, if many players are in the pot, you should play more hands, especially hands that have the potential to make big hands, such as straight and flush draws. This would include hands like:

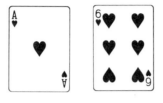

and

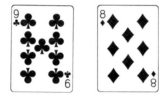

But normally you would only play these hands if the raiser were on your left.

We generally do not recommend that you call raises in the big blind with a hand like:

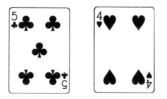

If this hand was suited then the call would be okay. But for these calls to be profitable, you usually need at least two ways to win. When the above hand is suited you have the two ways — a straight and a flush. But when it is not suited, there are not enough ways to come out on top. If your cards were higher, usually nine-eight or better, then you might be able to win if you flop a draw, miss it, but make a pair after the flop. Thus a call would now be correct since it is much easier to win the pot with something like a pair of nines than a pair of fives. To call with a small unsuited connecting hand you need to be against weak players who will not extract the maximum from you when you flop a draw, but who will frequently pay off if you make something.

When the pot is raised in early position and you are in the big blind, one hand that demands special attention is KJ. The reason for this is that a hand such as

can easily make a second-best hand that you will have to pay off all the way. This does not mean that you can never call a legitimate raise with KJ, but it does mean that the typical player calls much too often with this hand. Again, this is one of those situations where knowing your opponent can be a crucial factor in determining the correct decision. Similar comments apply for AJ, AT, and KT.

To call with a small pair you usually only need two players in. Thus

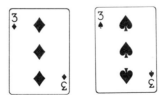

would be playable against an early position raiser and a caller. This should assure you the implied odds that are necessary in case you flop a set. And, of course, you usually would reraise with AA or KK when you are in either blind. But as already discussed, don't automatically reraise with AK (or QQ, for that matter).

.One situation where big-blind play changes drastically occurs when you are against a possible steal-raise — that is, a raise from a late position by a player who you think would attempt to pick up the blinds with a weak hand. Remember, against a legitimate raise, you still need a fairly good hand to call. In fact, a good guideline is to play essentially the same hands that you normally would cold call a raise or reraise with if you were in a late position. But a steal-raise is a different matter. Now you are forced to play more hands. How many more hands depends on the skill of your opponent. The worse he plays the more you play.

Against weak opponents who won't make good use of their positional advantage on the flop, you can call in the big blind with hands as weak as those in Group 8. However, it still might be best to throw some of the smaller non-suited connectors away. You should reraise about one-fourth of the time, usually with your best hands.

If someone calls in between you and your opponent, or if your opponent plays well, then you must tighten up some. But you still can play a lot of hands, perhaps Groups 1-6.

Many of these same comments also apply to the little blind. However, when you call a raise from the little blind, not only do you have to put a larger fraction of a bet into the pot, but also a player remains to act behind you. One situation where correct little-blind play differs from big-blind play is against a possible steal-raise. Now if you are going to play (usually with a hand in Groups 1-6), you should almost always reraise. The purpose of this reraise is to drive the big blind out of the pot. However, if someone else has already called the raise, then this play is usually incorrect without an excellent hand because you now know that at least one of your opponents is likely to have a legitimate hand. In addition, you should, as usual, consider how well your opponent plays. Remember, the better he plays, the higher quality hand you need to make this type of play.

There are two other spots where little-blind play differs from big-blind play. The first occurs when the pot is not raised and it will cost you only a fraction of a bet to play. If the fraction to enter the pot is half a bet, then you (the player in the little blind) should still be somewhat selective of the hands you play, though you should play loose. For example, hands like

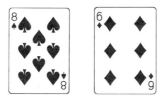

any two suited cards, or if the pot is short-handed, a hand that contains an ace, are *all* probably right to call with. But hands like

should still be thrown away. However, if it costs only one-third of a bet to enter the pot, every hand should be played. In this spot, it is just too cheap to throw away your hand, no matter how bad it is. The one exception occurs when the big blind is a frequent raiser. Why waste even one-third of a bet, since you have to fold if he raises.

If no one has raised, the pot is short-handed, you are in the small blind, and the big blind is apt to call your raise, you should only raise with your best hands. This generally means Group 1 and 2. On the other hand, if the big blind will fold a lot you should now raise with many more hands. This would include the Group 3 hands and those Group 4 hands made up of high ranking cards. However, when making this play with a marginal hand do not forget to consider your opposition. You should be less inclined to make this play against the better players.

If no one has raised, the pot is multiway, and you are in the small blind, only raise with the hands that are either very strong or some hands that play well multiway.

Remember, when you make this raise you are putting a lot of money in the pot out of position.

The other situation that is unique to the little blind is when everyone has thrown away their hands. The question now is whether to fold, call the big blind, or raise the big blind. In addition to the ideas in the previous paragraph, keep in mind that for all four betting rounds, you will be at a positional disadvantage to the big blind.

However, if the big blind throws away too many hands in this situation you should frequently raise. For example, in a $10-$20 game, it costs you $15 to raise when you have the little blind. There is $15 in the pot already. Therefore, if the big blind folds more than 50 percent of the time, you would show an immediate profit with any two cards. Add this to the fact that sometimes you will win when you are called, and it becomes worthwhile to raise when your chance of stealing the ante is as little as 30 percent. Few players in the big blind will discard their hands this often in this situation, but when you find one who will, you should take advantage of him.

To clarify this idea, here's an example. If you hold a hand like

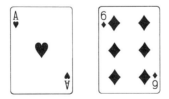

you should frequently just call. However, if the big blind folds a lot, or folds too much on the flop, you should always raise. (For more discussion see "Part Five: Playing Short-handed" which begins on page 183.)

Generally, if you are in the big blind, everyone passes to the small blind, and he raises, you normally need to make sure that you call enough so that the player in the little blind does not show an *automatic* profit. (Remember, this will be the case if you fold as little as 30 percent of the time.) On the other hand, if you know that this player has high raising standards, you should fold your weaker hands.

# The First Two Cards: Late-Position Blind

In most cardrooms, if you miss your blinds or have just entered a game, you are allowed to post what is known as a late-position blind. (A blind just to the right of the button.) If you are new to the game, you must post an amount equal to the big blind; if you have missed the blinds, you must post an amount equal to both the big and the little blinds. However, in both cases, only an amount equal to the big blind is live. (This late-position blind is posted in addition to the big and little blinds to the left of the dealer button.)

Because of your improved position and the increased amount of money in the pot, there are some significant strategy changes versus regular blind play. For instance, if everyone passes, you should raise with most of your hands. This is one of those situations where either folding or raising is the best play, while just calling is usually the worst option. But because you already have posted your blind, you cannot fold. This means that raising is usually correct. The exception is when you are against opponents who almost always will defend their blinds, no matter how poor their hands are.

If some players have already called, you would normally raise only with those hands that you usually raise with had you not posted a late-position blind. In fact, you may want to raise *less* often, since your opponents will now misread the strength of your hand.

Because of your position, if the pot is raised in front of you, you can call with a hand slightly worse than what you would play in the big blind. But you still must be very selective, especially if you are against a good player. Remember to distinguish between a legitimate raise and a possible steal-raise. Against the latter, it is probably okay to play with any ace and most kings, depending on how well your opponent plays. And if you do decide to play you should often reraise.

# The First Two Cards

# Afterthought

We have seen that in Texas hold 'em it is relatively easy to specify exactly how the first two cards should be played. This is because at this stage of play, proper strategy is not yet that complicated. This doesn't mean that you cannot make mistakes, but it does mean that if you understand the situation and have good judgment, it should be fairly clear as to what the correct play should be. Unfortunately, as we shall soon see, this is not always true with play on the flop and beyond.

We would also like to stress again that unless you are in the blind, you should not be calling many raises, particularly if the pot is short-handed. You should usually reraise or fold, with folding being much more prevalent. To do otherwise is the classic "weak player" mistake, and it is the easiest way to tell if an opponent does not understand the game as well as he should.

Another idea to keep in mind when playing hold 'em is that it is easy to become frustrated and to start playing too many hands. For example, a hand like

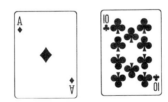

can begin to look almost as good as a hand like

In some situations, such as when you are in a steal position and no one has yet entered the pot, this is probably true. But in other spots, having the bigger kicker is crucial. If an ace flops, a queen should win where a ten may not. You are also much more likely to flop top pair with a queen than with a ten. In addition, if you do flop top pair with a queen rather than a ten, you don't have to worry as much about overcards hitting on a later round. This adds up to a lot of extra pots and extra money.

The ideas in this chapter are all very important. But even though playing your first two cards correctly is absolutely crucial to winning play, it will not automatically make you a winner. Perfect play on the first two cards will enable you to only break even at best if you are not adept at the later rounds. So read on.

# Part Two
# Strategic Concepts

# Strategic Concepts

# Introduction

Most of the profit in hold 'em comes from knowing how to play after the first round. Unfortunately, the game quickly becomes so complex that it is impossible to discuss every situation, which is why it's important to develop general strategic concepts to guide you toward winning play.

That is the purpose of this section. When you finish reading it, you should have a good idea of how to approach most situations at the hold 'em table. Although you still won't be an expert, as this additionally requires a great deal of experience, you should be well on your way toward achieving this goal.

Also, at this juncture, we would like to recommend a more general book on poker concepts, namely *The Theory of Poker* by David Sklansky. While not specifically about hold 'em, this book is must reading for all serious players.

# Semi-Bluffing

In *The Theory of Poker*, David Sklansky defines a semi-bluff as "a bet with a hand which, if called, does not figure to be the best hand at the moment, but has a reasonable chance of outdrawing those hands that initially called it." Notice that when you are semi-bluffing, there are two ways that you might win the pot. First, no one may call and you will win the pot immediately. Second, if you do get customers, you still may improve to the best hand. It is the combination of these two possibilities that makes this class of plays profitable, and as we shall see, semi-bluffing plays a crucial role in any winning hold 'em strategy. Also notice that the semi-bluff necessarily means that more cards are to come.

Obvious examples of semi-bluff situations in hold 'em are when you have flopped an inside straight draw, or second or third pair with an overcard kicker. In these examples, you would prefer that all of your opponents fold. However, if you are called, you still have a chance to win if the right card comes on the turn. A specific example of a semi-bluff situation is when you hold

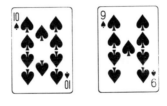

against not too many opponents, and the flop comes

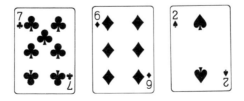

In this case, an eight will give you the absolute nuts, and a nine or a ten will give you an overpair (to the flop), which also may be good enough to win.

You might not want to semi-bluff when you are in last position. That is because you may be check-raised, and instead of seeing the next card for free, it will cost you two bets. Thus, the factor that determines whether to bet in this situation is often how frequently you think you will be check-raised. This is partially dependent on the opponents you are up against. Keep in mind that some players constantly will go for a check-raise, while other players seldom will make this play. (More discussion on this concept appears later in the text.)

On the other hand, your bet in this spot may buy you a free card on a succeeding round, which is another reason to semi-bluff. As usual, experience and knowledge of how your opponents play will help you make the right decisions in these situations.

Here is another example of a correct semi-bluff. You hold

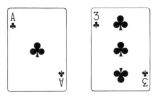

and the flop is

Notice that you have middle pair with the very best kicker, plus "back-door" flush potential. (Backdoor flush potential means that you will make a flush if both the fourth- and fifth-street cards are of your suit.) The correct play is to bet if you think you have any chance of winning the pot immediately. If you get called, you still can win if an ace or a trey comes on the turn. Against poor players who call too much, semi-bluffing may not be correct in this situation (although a bet might still be worth it, since you may have the best hand and will often be called with worse hands).

Following are some other examples of correct semi-bluffs. First, let's look at a four-flush or open-end straight draw — especially with a pair — with one card to come. Suppose you hold

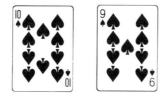

and the board is

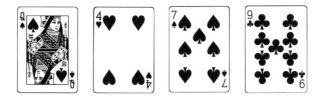

Notice that you have a pair plus a flush draw. This means that there are 14 cards left in the deck (out of the remaining 46 unseen cards) that will give you a strong hand. (If you had an open-end straight draw and a pair, there would be 13 cards left in the deck that would give you a strong hand.) This is usually enough potential, along with the possibility that all of your opponents may fold, to make a bet the correct move. If you do not have a pair — that is, you have only a straight draw (eight outs) or a flush draw (nine outs) — your hand is not as good. However, this does not mean that it is correct to check (and then call if there is a bet), but rather that you should bet only if you think there is a decent chance that all of your opponents will fold.

Let's look at the small pair with an overcard kicker. Suppose you have

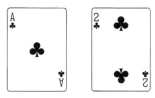

the flop is

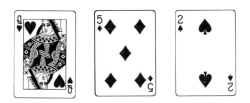

and there are six people in the pot. It is still correct to bet against typical players. However, it would be different if you had

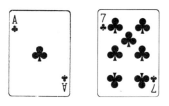

and the flop came

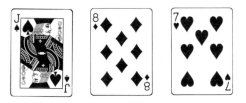

There is a good chance that other players would like this flop, as straight draws are now likely. Another example would be if the flop

comes with two suited cards. Once again be less inclined to semi-bluff, especially against a lot of opponents, since a flush draw will surely play against you.

Now suppose the flop is

and you hold

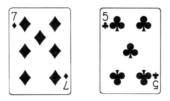

(giving you a "gut shot") against many opponents. This is another time when semi-bluffing is usually correct. However, if the flop comes

and you hold the same 7♦5♣, it is probably best not to semi-bluff, because with a ten-high flop, it is easy for two overcards to call. However, with a queen-high flop, an opponent must have precisely AK to have two overcards. That is, in the second example, it is much harder to win by betting, thus making a semi-bluff incorrect.

Here is a good rule to follow: If your hand is worth a call or even *almost* worth a call if you check, then it is better to bet if there is some chance that you can win the pot right there. Notice that we are not mentioning the fear of a raise on the flop, as the threat of a raise does not automatically stop us from semi-bluffing. This is because in today's structure, the bet on the flop is often very small when compared with the size of the pot. Of course, if you think there is a good possibility of being raised, then this is another matter. The criterion of having some chance of winning the pot immediately is diminished, and it would have been incorrect to semi-bluff to begin with.

A secondary advantage to semi-bluffing is that when you do make your hand, your opponent often will misread it. Suppose in the gut-shot draw example, you have 7♦5♣ and the flop is Q♣6♥3♦. Now a four comes on the next card. Who would dream that you have made a straight? If it turns out that you happen to be up against another strong hand, such as a set of sixes, you might get almost unlimited action.

A third advantage to semi-bluffing is that it keeps your opponents guessing. If you never bluff, you are simply giving away too much information. Players in this category are referred to as "weak tight." They are easy to make money against since you virtually always know exactly where they are, but they have a great deal of trouble figuring out what your hand is. Semi-bluffing is a good way to mix up your play so you can't be "read" as easily.

And finally, a fourth advantage of semi-bluffing, as we mentioned earlier, is that you may get a free card on the next round. This is especially true against timid players who are afraid to bet into anyone who has shown strength. (Keep in mind however that if you do take a free card you may be giving up your chance to bluff later, or you may get bluffed out yourself by encouraging someone else to bluff on the end.)

One last situation that we would like to address is how to play two overcards on the flop. Overcards frequently should be bet, especially if you have back-door flush potential, unless you think a reasonable chance exists that if you catch your card, you still won't win. Thus if a straight-type flop hits, or a flop with two suited cards, you would be less inclined to bet, especially against many opponents. However, if two suited cards flop and you have one of that suit and it is an ace or a king, betting is often right provided that you are against a small number of opponents. The same thing can be said when you have two suited high cards and one of those suits flop, even if the other two are another suit.

If you do bet two overcards and are raised, the question now is whether you should call. The answer, again, depends on what you think your chance of winning is if one of your overcards hits and on the pot odds you are getting. This is another spot where good judgment, experience, and knowledge of your opponent can help in determining your decision.

If someone else bets on the flop, is it correct to call with two overcards?[4] This also relates to your judgment concerning your chance of winning if one of your overcards hits and to your pot odds. Look at the texture of the flop. Specifically, be more inclined to call with a flop like

than with a flop like

---

[4]This concept does not really come under the heading of semi-bluff, but we include it here since we are talking about how to play two overcards on the flop.

Notice that with the second flop, you are more likely to be against two pair, as the typical player will enter a pot more often with a hand like

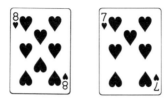

than with a hand like

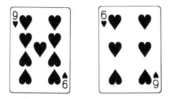

And if you do decide that your hand (two overcards) is worth playing (usually because of the chance that you will improve, plus the chance that you have the best hand), you should consider *raising* rather than calling. If nothing else, this play may get you a free card — a subject that is covered in the next chapter.

Finally, if small cards flop, be more inclined to call with KQ than with AK. This is because many more people play hands like Ax than Kx.

Here's an example. Before the flop two players limp in, you raise, and one of the blinds calls. The flop is:

You should be more inclined to call with

than with

Now if you get lucky and catch your pair, you are less likely to be against two pair.

# The Free Card

When you bet or raise on an early round in order to get checked to on the next round, you are not actually getting a free card. In reality, you are getting a card cheaply. If everything works, it appears as though you are getting a free card, but that "free" card cost you a bet on the previous round. If things do not work as hoped, the free card you are trying to get may become quite expensive. (Your opponent might reraise and then bet into you on fourth street.) However, there are many situations where trying for a cheap card is beneficial. (And from this point on we will refer to it as free since it is standard poker jargon.)

Since *getting* a free card is often advantageous when your hand is weak, it should be obvious that when you have a legitimate hand, it is usually to your disadvantage to *give* any free cards. Specifically, you should bet most of your legitimate hands to give your opponent a chance to drop. This includes holdings like four-flushes or open-end straight draws with two cards to come. By the way, be willing to bet open-end straight draws with two flush cards on board as long as there are two cards to come, unless you feel that there is a good chance that you will be raised. It is true that you may make your straight and run into a flush. But remember that it is often correct to bet on the flop with a small pair and an overcard, a hand that has only five cards that will improve it. Even if a flush draw is out, you still have six cards that will make your straight draw a winning hand, and many times that winning hand will be the "nuts." (Of course six outs against an opponent's flush draw is not as good as five outs against a non-flush draw since you can catch and still lose.)

You also usually should bet top pair or an overpair on the flop, as long as your hand figures to be the best hand. The exceptions are when there is a lot of raising before the flop (indicating that you may not have the best hand), and those times when you have decided to check-raise. (These topics are discussed in more detail later in the text.) Specifically, resist the inclination to check to the before-the-flop-raiser. Checking and calling is rarely a correct strategy in hold 'em, yet this is precisely the way that many weak opponents will play.

However, there are three situations where checking and calling may be correct. The first occurs when you are slowplaying. (See "Slowplaying" on page 73.) The second situation is when you are fairly sure that your opponent has a better hand and will not fold if you bet, but the pot odds justify your calling in the hope that either you have the best hand or you may outdraw your opponent. The third situation is when you are against a habitual bluffer. Now, even though you risk giving a free card, checking and calling is probably the best strategy to follow.

Another interesting concept is that even when you are a big favorite and want callers, but you think everyone will fold if you bet, giving a free card still may be incorrect. In this case, the next card might be a miracle card for someone else, but not likely to make anyone a second-best hand. An obvious example of this can be seen when you flop a small flush. A check could give someone else a higher flush, and that person would not have called your bet. Specifically, suppose you hold

and three spades flop. If you bet, someone with the 8♠, 9♠, T♠, or J♠ most likely will throw his hand away. If you check and a fourth spade comes, you may have cost yourself the pot.

These examples illustrate the general principle of free cards. That is, if you check and allow someone who would not have called your bet to outdraw you, then you have allowed a "mathematical catastrophe" to happen. It is also a catastrophe to give a free card to someone who would have called your bet, and he fails to outdraw you. However, this second mathematical catastrophe is not as bad as the first. It can also be beneficial to give this free card if it makes someone misplay their hand.

There are four other basic situations where it is correct to check on the flop. The first is when you are sure that you do not have the best hand and especially sure that you will be called if you bet. This frequently will occur when you have several opponents and the board flops either three cards that rank close to each other or two suited cards.

For instance, suppose you have

you are against several opponents, and the flop is

It is usually wrong to bet. There is little chance that everyone will fold, and you have almost no chance of improving to the best hand.

The second situation where it is generally correct to check is when you think it is likely that someone behind you will bet. This often occurs when you are in a two or three-person pot and were raised by an aggressive opponent before the flop. Some of these players automatically will bet on the flop when you check to them, no matter which cards have come.

When this is the case and you have flopped a strong hand, almost always go for a check-raise. In fact, with a non-threatening flop, you sometimes should check-raise and then bet again on fourth street even when you have nothing. (However, don't get carried away with this play. Make it only occasionally.)

The third situation where it is correct to check is with a hand that should be slowplayed. But we want to add that one of the deciding factors as to whether to slowplay is not just the strength of your hand but also the chance that the *next card* will make someone else a second best hand.

Finally, when you have flopped top pair, either aces or kings, and you have a weak kicker it might be right to check and call. Notice that if you don't have the best hand, you save money by not having to call any raise. Also notice (and this is extremely important) that few free cards can hurt you. Specifically, when you have aces and, to a lesser degree, kings, you are not worried about overcards beating you.

But suppose you have flopped top pair, not aces or kings, and you have a weak kicker. (This usually happens when you get a "free" play in the big blind.) How should this hand be played?

The answer is somewhat complex. Against a small number of opponents, you should bet so you are not giving a free card that could easily beat you. Against a large number of opponents, you should check and perhaps fold especially if it is bet in early position and you have players behind you yet to act. This is because with several players still to act, it is unlikely that the bettor would bet a hand that you could beat. (The pot is said to be "protected.") Few players will bluff in this spot. Though your opponent may be betting a draw, the combination of factors should deter you from calling, unless the pot is offering very good odds.

But if the bet comes from a late-position player after you have checked to a large number of opponents, you should raise. Even though you don't always hold the best hand, there is a good chance that you do, and by getting the pot heads-up, you will maximize your chance of winning.

Here's an example. Suppose the flop is

No one raised before the flop, many players are in the pot, and you are in the blind with a queen and a weak kicker. You should check, and if a late-position player bets, you should raise (regardless of your kicker.) You are trying to restrict the competition to a small number of players, most likely just you and the bettor, and since he bet after all or most of the other players checked there is a good chance that you have the best hand.

However, you must be cautious if you have top pair (with a weak kicker) that is below queens. This is especially true against tough players for a little-known reason that normally is considered only by experts.

The principle is that it is more probable for someone else to have top pair in an unraised pot when the top card is a jack or lower. This is because good players are more likely either to raise or fold when they have an ace, king, or queen in their hands (depending on their other card) and less likely to just call. Thus, when nobody raises before the flop, a flop like

is not likely to make a pair of kings for someone else.[5] So if you played

in the blind, you should like your hand. However, if you hold

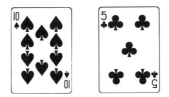

and the flop is

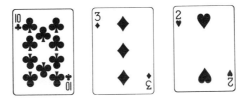

you must fear the possibility of a ten — unraised pot or not — since most players will just call with a hand like:

---

[5]This principle of course does not hold true for loose wild games where players routinely play Kx offsuit.

or

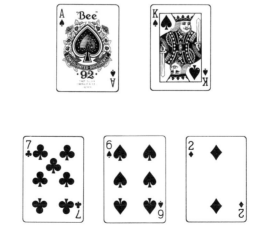

In this case, unless you have a good kicker, or the pot is quite large, or you have a back-door flush draw, you usually should fold top pair when that top pair is jacks or lower. (However, if you do play, you generally should raise.)

One concept that we already have stressed is that you should avoid checking decent hands to the before-the-flop raiser in most situations. But most players do check. So if you are the before-the-flop raiser in a multiway pot, your hand is weak, and everyone checks to you, you almost always should take a free card rather than bet someone else's hand. But under the same circumstances in a short-handed pot, you should usually bet because there is a reasonable chance that you can win the pot right there.

Following is an example of this concept. Suppose you hold

the flop is

and everyone checks to you. If the pot is being played short-handed, you should bet. The main reason for this is that you don't want to give a free card to someone holding a hand like:

This bet also might gain you a free card on the next round. In fact, betting or raising in late position with a hand that does not seem to justify it is sometimes correct if you think this may cause your opponent to allow a card to drop off at no further charge. However, keep in mind that if you take the free card, some opponents automatically will bet on the river, no matter what they have or what the last card is. Against these types of players, it is frequently necessary to call with as little as ace high after you have shown weakness by checking on fourth street.

If you hold the A♠K♠ in the above example and you don't bet the flop after it is checked to you be prepared to bet the turn not only if an ace or king hits, but also as a bluff if a queen or perhaps a jack hits. If a small card hits and it is checked to you don't bet in a loose game since it will be very unlikely that you can pick up the pot. But in a tight game this bet may be correct. By the way, this play would be even stronger if your hand is QJ (since they fear AK). You will now have six legitimate cards to bet — your pair cards, and eight cards to bluff with.

It is also frequently correct to raise in late position on the flop with a four-flush. If the game is not tough — that is, you do not fear a reraise and your raise will encourage your opponents to check to you on the next round — you should raise more than half the time. However, you want players with this type of flop. Consequently, if there is a bet and several players remain to act behind you, it is often better to just call. (You still should consider raising if the pot is large, especially if you have overcards.)

Incidentally, even if you can't get a free card with your flush draw, since the odds against making your hand are approximately 2-to-1, your raise is also correct if you are sure that at least three players will call. But not if a pair flopped. In this case, you can make your flush and still lose the pot, so you usually should just call. (See "Part Three: Miscellanious Topics" — "Staying With a Draw" on page 117.)

Keep in mind that any time you are in a late position on the flop and have a hand that is worth a call, you should seriously consider raising. In fact, sometimes it is worth raising when you are absolutely sure that the bettor has you beat.

Here's an example. Suppose that five players have put in three bets each before the flop. You are in last position with

and are sure that no one has aces or kings since you put in the last raise. The flop is:

If the player to your right bets after everyone else has checked, you should raise, even if you are sure that he has two tens. Since the pot has become very large, it is important that you maximize your chance of winning it, even if you often cost yourself a few more bets. In the example given, your raise on the flop probably has increased your chance from about 15 percent (had you just called) to about 25 percent. By knocking people out, you have made it more likely that you will win if a queen or a jack comes. Though this play may cost you more money, it is well worth it. Additionally, it may *save* you money if your raise has scared the bettor into just calling and then checking on fourth street. As far as your back-door flush and straight chances are concerned, you probably would win with these hands, even if you let everybody in. However, the extra back-door chances are what made it wrong to fold originally, and as we've just shown, if you don't fold, it is better to raise.

Here is another example of how back-door potential can improve your hand and make a raise correct. Suppose you have

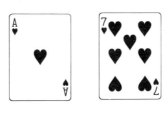

and the flop is

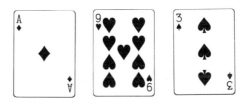

Notice that the flop includes an ace and one of your suit. If someone else bets, you should raise. Now bet on the turn with the intention of just showing down on the river if you do not improve. If you get check-raised on fourth street, you usually should fold, unless you helped or picked up a flush draw. You don't have enough chance to draw out against a legitimate hand to make it worth calling the check-raise. But if your opponent may be bluffing or semi-bluffing, you've got to keep him honest. Had you not flopped a three-flush with your pair of aces, a raise on the flop is less likely to be correct. In fact, without the back-door flush potential, it may be better to fold.

# Slowplaying

Slowplaying basically means to play a hand weakly on one round of betting in order to *lure* people in for later bets. Hands that are correct to slowplay don't come up very often. For a slowplay to be correct the following criteria must be met:

1. Your hand must be very strong.
2. You probably will chase everyone out by betting, but you have a good chance of winning a large pot if you check.
3. The free card that you are giving has good possibilities of making second-best hands.
4. This free card has little chance of making a better hand for someone or even of giving him a draw to a better hand with sufficient odds to justify a call.
5. The pot must not yet be very large.

An example of a possible correct slowplay is to check a set of jacks when the flop comes

Notice that in this example, an overcard on fourth street can easily give someone a second-best hand. Conversely, with a lot of opponents, someone could pick up a flush draw or an open-end straight draw on the turn and could then beat you on the end. So even here, slowplaying may not be correct if the pot has become large (or if several bad players, who may call your bet with as little as one overcard, are in the pot.)

Keep in mind that if the situation is not perfect, slowplaying is almost never correct. For example, if the flop is

and you have

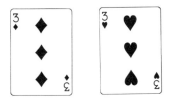

you usually should bet or raise on the flop, as your opponents can hold many possible hands, including flush and straight draws.

Another time that you generally should not slowplay is when you have flopped the absolute nuts. (Exception: When you have all the good cards; for example you hold A7 and the flop is A77.) This is because an opponent also may have flopped a very strong hand and will give you plenty of action. For instance, don't slowplay the nut flush if there is a chance that someone else also may have flopped a flush. If he is slowplaying, you will have cost yourself a lot of money.

Remember that for slowplaying to be correct, your opponents must have the opportunity to make a good second-best hand. As an example, if you hold two aces and a third ace flops, it is generally correct to bet and pick up the pot. In this case, there is usually not a second-best hand for your opponents to make, but a miracle card could cause you to lose the pot. (Of course a check is right if you think it will entice a bluff.)

A strategy similar to slowplaying is to just call someone else's bet in order to reraise a raiser behind you or to go for a raise on fourth street when the bet is twice as large. To do this, your hand must be almost as strong as a regular slowplaying hand.

For instance, when you flop top two pair and the player on your immediate right bets into you. You may want to wait until the turn to raise. That is, just call on the flop. This play is optimal if you are sure that this player will bet again. However, should a third player raise behind you, it is probably better to reraise on the flop and gain extra bets from all your opponents.

Here's an example. Suppose you limp in with

you are raised by an aggressive player behind you, and a player in the blind calls. Now suppose the flop is

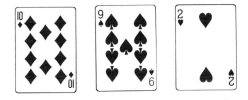

and the player in the blind leads out. You should just call with the intention of raising him on fourth street. However, if the original raiser now raises behind you, you usually should go ahead and reraise. This would be especially true if this opponent is the type of player who would raise with two overcards hoping to get a free card.

# Check-Raising

Check-raising is the play of checking your hand with the intention of raising on the same round after an opponent bets. Notice that check-raising and slowplaying are two ways of playing a strong hand weakly to trap your opponents. However, they are not the same thing. In addition, the check-raise should often be used to exclude opponents from competing for the pot. Sometimes, in limit hold'em, this is the most desirable characteristic of check-raising.

For check-raising to be correct, you usually should:

1. Think you have the best hand (though not a slowplaying hand).
2. Be quite sure that someone will bet behind you if you check.

A situation where check-raising probably would be correct is when you flop top two pair, there are many players on the flop, and you are in an early position. This is especially true if you think that the bet will come from a late position player. (The action before the flop will frequently indicate where the bet is likely to come from.)

Sometimes it is also correct to check-raise with a drawing hand. An example is when you think a player to your left will bet and two or more players will call. However, don't raise if you fear a reraise or if a reasonable chance exists that your hand won't win even if you hit it (perhaps a pair shows). Also keep in mind that a four-flush or an open-end straight draw normally should be bet if there is any chance that you can steal the pot.

Two interesting things may happen if you check a lot of good hands on the flop. First, some of your opponents may become afraid to bet. That is, they may be more inclined to give you a free card, and this free card may win the pot for you. Second, even if a blank hits on the turn, you now may be able to steal the pot. Your opponents are not going to suspect a bluff merely because you didn't bet on the flop, as they know you might have been trying for a check-raise. In fact, some of your opponents might feel smug when you bet, since they "escaped your trap." (When you are bluffing in this situation, never show your hand.) However, remember that if you check a lot of hands on the flop, the free card that you give occasionally may cost you the pot.

You also can check-raise semi-bluff. For example, suppose you have

and the flop comes

You bet and are raised, and you (correctly) call the raise. The next card is the

Now the correct play is for you to check-raise. You want your opponent to fold, but with your straight-flush draw, you have a lot of outs even if you are called.

Here is another example. Suppose you hold

and the flop comes

If any spade hits on fourth street, you can try for a check-raise. This is probably the right play whether or not you were raised on the flop. However, if your opponent is a "caller," it may be best to simply bet.

There is another very important reason to check-raise. It may be the most important. It is the fact that in games of today's structure, the bet on the flop is often not large enough, when compared to the size of the pot, to make it incorrect for drawing hands (and this includes hands like middle pair) to call. This means that you should check-raise a fair amount of time in an attempt to cut down the odds for opponents to draw out on you when the pot is large. (If the pot is small you should be more inclined to bet your good hands, your draws, and your semi-bluffs.)

A good guideline to follow is to consider check-raising if it is unlikely that an overcard can hurt you. That is, if you flop top pair and your top pair is aces, kings, or queens (and you have an overcard kicker with your queen), check-raising is often the correct play, especially if several players remain to act behind you. If your top pair is lower than queens, it is more dangerous to try for a check-raise, since a free card can easily beat you.

On the other hand, if you flop top pair in a large multiway pot, it still may be correct to check-raise, even if you are afraid of an overcard, especially if you are in an early position. This is because the pot is now so large that if you bet, you can expect a lot of callers anyway. Consequently, in an effort to thin the field, it may be necessary to risk the dreaded free card.

Here's an example. You are in an early position and hold

in a large multiway pot. The flop comes:

You must consider going for a check-raise. If you bet into many players and the pot is large, you probably will get several callers, and an ace or a king is likely to beat you. But if you go for a check-raise and are able to isolate a late-position player, you still may win even if one of those cards hits. Your check-raise also is likely to force out hands such as 87, while a simple bet wouldn't. Now you've eliminated the 1-in-5 chance that a player holding this type of hand will beat you.

One other thing to consider is how aggressive your opponents are and whether your hand is strong enough for three bets. For example, if you flop a very strong hand and a very aggressive player who showed some preflop strength is in late position, it might be best to lead and go for three bets, by reraising his raise.

# Odds and Implied Odds

Most players make many of their calling decisions based on the size of the pot compared to the current bet. This is called pot odds. While this does give an indication of what is correct, pot odds should be adjusted based on the expected future action of your opponents. For example, if the bettor is to your right and there are other players who might raise behind you, you should adjust the pot odds considerably lower. This means you have to fold more hands.

Here are two extreme examples of this concept. First, suppose you hold

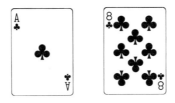

and the flop is

If a solid player to your right bets, a number of players are behind you, and there has been no raise before the flop, you should *fold*. Notice that in this example, not only might you be against a better ace, but a spade or a straight card can beat you. (Against a "loose bettor" who would play any ace, and bet any ace or queen, you should raise rather than fold. You should also continue to play against a player who will only bet a draw, and check his better hands hoping to get in a check-raise.) But against most bettors you should simply fold.

A second example is to fold in the same situation if you hold

and the flop is

(Again notice that you can be against a better jack, or that a spade or straight card can beat you.)

Other exceptions to folding these hands are when the pot has become very large and/or the game is very loose. Also, remember that calling is sometimes the worst play. That is, folding or raising in these situations is usually the superior strategy. If the pot is large and you are going to play, it is generally correct to raise with these types of hands. You should seldom call, as you cannot afford to give someone behind you who holds a marginal hand the correct odds to draw out.

There are cases such as when the board is the J♠T♠8♥ shown above, where if you have decided to play it may be best to call. If the scare card does come, you can throw your hand away. But if a blank arrives, you raise to thin out the field.

In addition, if you call on the flop and intend to also call on fourth street, keep in mind that the pot odds you are getting are not as good as they appear. The additional call that you plan to make lowers the effective odds that you are receiving from the pot. (For a more detailed discussion of these concepts, see *The Theory of Poker* by David Sklansky.)

Sometimes, however, the opposite will be the case. That is, your odds actually are better than the odds that the pot is offering you. This occurs when you plan to continue playing only if you hit your hand. Otherwise, you will fold. What this means is that the pot does not have to offer you seemingly correct odds to play a particular hand. That is because it is offering you implied odds.

An example is to call before the flop with a small pair, getting as low as 5-to-1 odds as long as there is little fear of a raise behind you. (The odds against flopping a set are approximately 7½-to-1.) Against players who give a lot of action, you can make this call even if you are getting a bit less than 5-to-1.) A second example is to try for an inside straight on the flop when you have odds of only about 8-to-1. (The odds against making your gut shot are approximately 11-to-1.)

Say, if you hold

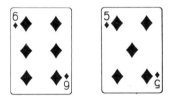

and the flop is

you can call even if you are getting a little less than the required 11-to-1. However, if a two flush is on board, or for some other reason you are not sure that your hand will be good if you hit it, you probably would want odds of at least 11-to-1 to call.

Finally, even if the odds don't seem to justify it, you still should make a loose call every now and then, as you don't want to become known as a "folder." If you are regarded as a folder, other players will try to run over you, and otherwise predictable opponents may turn tricky and become difficult to play against. (Once again, for a more thorough analysis of pot odds and implied odds, see *The Theory of Poker* by David Sklansky.)

# Bluffing

Bluffing is the act of betting on the last round when you are quite sure that you do not have the best hand, or on an earlier round when you have little chance of making the best hand. When you bluff, you are hoping that your opponent will fold. Typically, you should bluff when you think the size of the pot, compared to the estimated probability that your opponent will fold, is large enough to make this play profitable (in terms of long-run expectation). For example, if there is $50 in the pot and the bet is $10, you are getting 5-to-1 odds on your bluff. In this situation, if you think your opponent will fold more than one time in six, bluffing would be correct.

Sometimes you should bluff even if the pot odds do not justify it, as this makes it more difficult for your opponent to read your hands in the future. (While this is an excellent play against a merely good player, realize that an expert player will probably be perceptive enough to understand what you are doing.)

Here is an example of a good fifth-street bluff: Suppose that you have only one opponent remaining, you are trying for a straight, and a third suited card appears on board. Against a player who is capable of folding, you may want to attempt a bluff. Specifically, suppose you started with

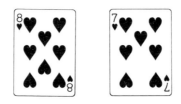

and on fifth street, the board is

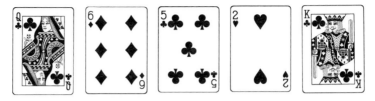

Whether you have been betting or calling up to this point, you should now consider betting if you are against a player who is capable of folding.

Sometimes the situation arises when you have very little, but still may have the best hand. Rather than check, it may be more beneficial to bet, just in case your bet makes an opponent fold a better hand. Occasionally this play works even more to your advantage when someone holding a worse hand calls. In a multiway pot, you may accomplish both objectives, which is the best result of all. As an example, suppose you are in an early position against a small number of players. Everyone checks on the flop and on fourth street. The board now pairs on fifth street, and you have a small pair or a hand like:

In this situation it is unlikely that the fifth-street card helped anyone. So if you bet and are called, you still may win the pot. Meanwhile, you may have forced someone else to fold a better hand.

An obvious example of a fourth-street bluff occurs when you are in a late position and everyone has checked on both the flop and fourth street. Now there is a good chance that a bet will win the pot right there, no matter what you have.

Another fourth street bluff occurs when you had bet the flop with either a draw or very little, and the top card on board pairs. If you weren't raised on the flop, this is a good spot to bet again.

A good bluffing opportunity also arises on the flop in a short-handed pot when no one has shown any strength before the flop. Suppose that you are in an early position — perhaps you were given a free play in the big blind — and the flop comes either ace high or king high with no flush or straight draws. A bet here should steal the pot often enough to make it profitable. This is especially true if, as already mentioned, you are in a game where most players tend to raise with better hands containing an ace or a king, and to throw away the other ace and king hands.

Specifically, flops like

are excellent candidates for this type of bluff. Remember, you want to be in early position, and you want the pot to be small.

Finally, a word must be said regarding when you should call an opponent who might be bluffing. If all the cards are out and your hand can beat only a bluff, your decision simply depends on your pot odds and on your judgment concerning the chance that your opponent is bluffing. If your hand can beat some of the hands he would bet for value as well as his bluffs you obviously do not need as great a "price" from the pot to make a call the right play.

# Inducing Bluffs

The ability to induce bluffs is a sign of an expert player. The idea is to manipulate your opponent into betting a hand that he originally had no intention of betting. These situations usually occur when you have a good calling hand. Consequently, since you plan to call anyway, you want to make sure that your opponent bets as often as possible those times when you hold the better hand.

Usually, these plays are accomplished by making what seems to be an otherwise irrational check, and they work best when you are against an aggressive player. A well-known example occurs when you hold either AA or KK and raise in last position before the flop. Now suppose the flop comes with a medium or small pair. It is checked to you, you bet, and a tough player calls. On fourth street, the correct play is often to check behind your opponent if he checks again. Notice that if he has flopped a set, your check probably will save you money. But, if he has no pair, you may get him to bluff at the pot on the end. The result is that you have gained an extra bet, since he likely would not have called your bet on the turn. (By the way, you would not want to make this play with a hand like JJ since too many overcards that could beat you might hit on the end.)

A similar example is when you have AA or KK and the top card on board pairs on the turn. Against a tough but aggressive player who check called you on the flop, check behind him if he doesn't bet.

Before inducing a bluff, several criteria have to be met. First, you usually should be facing only a small number of opponents, preferably just one. Second, you need to be against a player who is capable of bluffing but also capable of folding if you bet. This is why you want your opponent to be the tough but aggressive type. And most important, the situation must be such that giving a free card to your opponent is not dangerous if his hand is worse than yours.

Here is a second example of this type of play. Suppose you hold

and raise from a late position. You are reraised by the player in the big blind, and the flop comes

Your opponent bets and you call. On fourth street, a blank hits and your opponent checks. You also should check with the intention of betting or calling on the river. Notice that if your opponent has a better hand than you have, you avoid being check-raised. Consequently, if your opponent cannot beat an ace, there is a good chance that he will either bet or call on the river when he might have folded on fourth street if you had bet your hand.

A third example is somewhat different, because it requires a multiway pot. Suppose you are in a late position, against several opponents. A fourth suited card hits on the turn, you have the king of that suit making you a flush, and everyone has checked to you. The correct play may be for you to also check. If you bet, you may not get any calls, plus if the ace of the appropriate suit is in one of your opponents' hands, you save money. However, by checking, you may induce a bluff, and if you don't induce a bluff, someone who would not have called on the turn may now call on the river.

For example, suppose you hold

in a multiway pot, and you are on the button. The flop comes

and the turn card is the

If no one bets, strongly consider checking. (If someone bets on fifth street, call.) If it is checked to you on fifth street, always bet; and if you now get checked-raised, always call unless you are sure your opponent wouldn't raise without the nuts. Remember, your check on fourth street may encourage someone to take a shot at you when you bet on the river.

Finally, we want to remind you once again that a fuller treatment of both bluffing and inducing bluffs can be found in *The Theory of Poker* by David Sklansky.

# Folding When the Pot is Big

In hold 'em, situations sometimes develop where it is virtually impossible for your opponent to be bluffing. Consequently, even though the pot may be quite large, it is frequently correct to throw away your hand.

As an example, suppose the pot is many-handed and you get a free play in the big blind. You hold

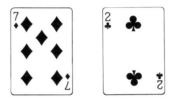

and the flop comes

You check, planning to check-raise, but no one bets. The fourth-street card is the

Again you check, planning to check-raise. And this time one player does bet, another calls, and you check-raise, limiting the pot to just

the three of you. On fifth street, another queen hits. Even though the pot is large, the correct play now is to check and fold, since at least one of your opponents will almost always have you beaten — probably by three queens.

# Heads-Up Versus Multiway

Keep in mind that many of the fancy plays we have been talking about do not work well when you are against a lot of opponents. In fact, making some of these plays in multiway pots will cost you money in the long run. Specifically, against many opponents, you should slowplay less, if at all, semi-bluff less, avoid bluffing — especially on the end against more than two opponents — and avoid inducing bluffs with checks that give free cards.

On the other hand, with many players in the pot, your implied odds usually have increased. This means that you are much more apt to play and even raise with small pairs, suited connectors, and hands like:

Conversely, when you hold big unsuited cards, your opponents are getting implied odds from *you*. Therefore, it is wrong to raise with unsuited high cards in multiway pots, and it may be right to fold hands like AT, KT, and even AJ and KJ.

Specifically, if you hold

on the button, and five or six players have limped in, you should strongly consider folding. Raising with this hand — which is a mistake frequently made by beginning players — will cost you money in the long run. Even calling might be wrong for all but the best players.

On the flop many hands play differently depending on the size of the pot and the number of players in the pot. Here's an example. Suppose you start with

the flop is

and the player on your right bets into you. If the pot is small you may only want to call. This is because the bettor may already have you beat and if you raise you won't lose someone who has flopped a four-flush. What you will knock out is a hand like middle pair or a gut shot draw. If the pot is big, you would now want to make this raise since anyone holding these hands may now be getting the correct odds to call.

You would also sometimes adjust your play if you flop a draw. Suppose in the above hand you held two small diamonds instead of the A♠K♣. As previously discussed, if the pot is small and you are first to act you should usually bet right out in the hopes that you might win it right there. If the pot is big, it might be correct to check and hope that the bet comes on your left, then you can check-raise and build a big pot. (However, this play is not recommended in tough games. One reason is that you are now more likely to be up against a bigger flush draw. The other reason is that in tough games the original bettor is more likely to reraise.) If the bet comes from a late position player you should probably just call and let the other players in behind you.

# Raising

There are five basic reasons to raise in hold 'em:
1. To get more money in the pot.
2. To drive players out.
3. To bluff (or semi-bluff).
4. To get a free card.
5. To gain information.

If you think you have the bettor beat, it is generally correct to raise, even if you risk driving out players behind you. In fact, in many cases, it is very important to drive out players on the flop. This is because in today's modern structure, the size of the pot is often so large in relation to the bet on the flop that it sometimes becomes correct to draw to long-shot hands if there is no raise (on the flop). Consequently, your raise in these spots often will save the whole pot for you.

By the way, if you are raising on the flop to drive people out, it usually will work only against those players who have not yet had a chance to call the original bet. It is a rare player who will fold his hand on the flop for one more bet after he already has put money into the pot. (Sometimes, however, the original bettor will help you drive out players by reraising.)

Even if you are not sure that you have the best hand, a raise is often correct. Keep in mind that if you do hold the best hand, or if your hand becomes the best hand, your raise may have stopped other opponents from drawing out on you.

Here's an example of raising with a probable second-best hand. Suppose you raised before the flop with

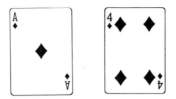

and the flop is

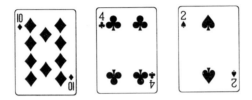

Notice that you have a pair and an overcard, plus back-door straight and back-door flush potential. If someone on your right bets, a raise is often correct, especially if you think that the raise will buy you a free card.

In very tough games, raising as a pure bluff can be occasionally done because players are capable of folding in big pots without calling one last bet. An example of this type of play is when one player bets and another calls on the river. If the right cards are out — especially if a scare card that is unlikely to help either of your opponents hits on the river — you can raise. This raise often works against the right players since there is a caller, who obviously is not bluffing. Thus it looks as though you must have something to make this play.

These plays usually are not recommended simply because they succeed rarely and are expensive when they fail. However, if the conditions are perfect and you know your opponents well, you occasionally may find an opportunity to pull this play off successfully.

The one time that you can bluff-raise in a weaker game is when you think your opponent is bluffing, but also think your hand is even worse. An example is when your flush draw did not get there, but the hand was played in such a fashion that you are fairly sure your opponent was also on a flush draw.

Here's an example of this play. Suppose you start with

and the flop is

An opponent bets, and you call. This opponent does not have a history of trying to check-raise. A blank hits on fourth street, and both you and your opponent check. Notice that there is a good chance that he is also on a flush draw and was betting on the flop in an attempt to pick up the pot. If another blank hits on the river and he bets, you may want to raise. If he was on a flush draw, you will probably win the pot.

You also can raise as a *semi*-bluff. For example, suppose you have

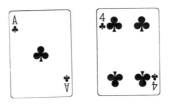

the flop is

and everyone checks. If the next card is the

giving you the nut flush draw and a gut-shot straight draw, you should usually raise if someone bets.

A similar opportunity to raise sometimes occurs in a short-handed pot when everyone checks on the flop and fourth street does not bring an overcard or three to a straight or flush. However, it gives you either a flush draw or an open-end straight draw. Now suppose an early-position player, who you know would try to steal in this spot, bets. Your correct play is to raise in the hope that your opponent will fold. But if he does not fold, you still have outs.

Here's an example of this play. You start with

and the flop is

No one bets, and the turn card is the

giving you an open-end straight draw. If an early-position player bets, and he is the type of player who would try to pick up the pot with no hand, you should go ahead and raise. If he calls with a legitimate hand, you still have at least eight outs to win.

Another opportunity for a semi-bluff raise occurs almost any time that you pick up a back-door flush draw after calling on the flop with a pair. But again, make this play only against someone who you think is capable of folding. And how likely is it that someone will fold for a raise? The answer is based on the answers to the following three questions:

1.    How capable is this person of folding a big hand?
2.    How likely is he to be semi-bluffing? (Of course, this is a matter of watching your opponent and learning exactly how he plays.)
3.    How are you perceived by this particular individual? Specifically, if other players think you virtually never bluff, you are more likely to get away with this play than if they think you are a wild and reckless player.

Raising to get a free card is best done when you are in late position and the bet is smaller than the bets on succeeding rounds. But, any hand that is worth a call is conceivably worth a raise.

Finally, raising to gain information should be done only rarely, usually just in heads-up situations. Even in the most favorable spots, this raise probably is not worth it, as you usually have to "pay" too much for the information. However, if your hand may be worth a raise anyway, the fact that you will gain information (based on how your opponent responds to your raise) might make raising the right play.

The best time to raise for information is against an opponent whose reaction to your raise will well define his hand. That is, depending on his play you will know for certain whether your hand is best.

Here's an example. You have

and an ace flops. You want to raise someone who will only reraise if your hand is no good. However, if you fold when you are reraised you need to be correct virtually every time.

# Heads-Up on Fifth Street

Many pots in hold 'em, even though they may start with a lot of players, often end up as two-player contests by the time all the cards are out. Consequently, on the end, you sometimes must apply concepts that are totally different from those that were operative in earlier betting rounds. This section provides some guidelines on how to proceed. First, let's discuss those situations where you are last to act.

The first question that many players ask is when is it correct to bluff? The answer is that if your hand probably can't win by checking, and the odds you are getting from the pot compared to the chance your opponent will call are favorable, then a bluff will be profitable.

This concept was addressed in an earlier section, so we won't go into detail again. But a lot depends on whether you have been the bettor or the caller. If you have been calling all the way, only a significant card that appears to help you but does not, such as a flush card on fifth street, may make a bluff correct. If, on the other hand, you have been betting all the way, you might try a bluff on the end regardless of the last card. Also, as has been emphasized in the text, remember to consider whether your opponent is capable of folding a decent hand.

One mistake that inexperienced players make is to bet when all the cards are out, simply because they think they have the best hand. The trouble with this play is that while you may have the best hand the majority of the time, your bet may still be a loser. That is, *when you are called*, your bet will lose the majority of the time — even though you expect to have the winning hand in a showdown. In fact, if your opponent has already checked, you should think you have the best hand at least 55 percent of the time *that you are called* for your bet to be correct (51 percent is not good enough because of the possibility that you will be check-raised).

Here are a couple of examples. First, suppose you have

and are against one opponent. The flop comes queen high, with or without two suited cards. If two blanks hit and the action has not been too heavy, you should bet on the river. It is very likely that a lesser hand will call you.

As a second example, suppose everything is the same as before except that the river card pairs the queen. If it is checked to you, a bet is now more dangerous but probably still correct. But if the last queen makes three of the suit, two of which flopped, then a bet would be wrong, even though you still have a reasonable chance to win the pot. A bet in this situation is wrong not only because you are less likely to win, but also because you are less likely to be called by a worse hand.

Specifically, if the board on fifth street is

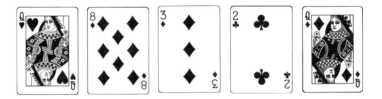

you normally should not bet. Although you still may have the best hand, if you are called, it is unlikely that your hand is good. (If your opponent has come out betting, you should call only if your chances compare favorably with the pot odds. This is often a function of knowing your opponent well and having lots of playing experience.)

Now here is an example of when a call is almost always correct. Suppose you have top pair, you have been betting all the way after your opponent has checked to you on each round, and the lowest card on board pairs on the river. Suddenly, to your surprise, your opponent bets. The question you must ask yourself is this: What could your opponent have been calling with? Is bottom pair a likely candidate? If it is reasonably possible that your opponent has bottom pair, why wouldn't he try to check-raise you on the end when this seemingly innocent card hit? Notice that there is clearly enough doubt in this situation that when the size of the bet is compared to the size of the pot, a call is usually the correct play against all but the most predictable opponents.

When you are planning to raise, you usually need to be about a 2-to-1 favorite to have the best hand on the end (except for bluff-raises) because of the possibility that you may be reraised and the fact that you might not get called unless you are beat. A raise is generally correct when you think you will have the best hand 55 percent of the time that your raise is called. (The two statements above are not contradictory. Do you see why?)

However, there is an interesting exception to this rule. If you think that your opponent probably has the same hand as you and you believe that your raise will sometimes make him fold, then you should raise every time. If he does have the same hand, this raise may win you half the pot. Even if he occasionally beats you out of that extra bet, this raise can still be worth it as long as he sometimes folds when his hand is the same as yours.

When you are first to act, you should always keep in mind what options you have in heads-up, last round situations. These options are:
1.  To bet.
2.  To check with the intention of folding.
3.  To check with the intention of calling.
4.  To check with the intention of raising.

When you have a good hand, whether to check-raise or come right out betting depends on three probabilities. They are:
1.  The chance that you will be called if you bet, assuming that you won't be raised.

2.    The chance that your opponent will bet if you check, but will not call your raise.

3.    The chance that he will bet and then call your raise.

Going for a check-raise becomes the correct strategy if the second probability added to twice the third probability exceeds the first probability. Needless to say, this is one of those situations where good judgment will come into play, as you will not have the time to make the appropriate probability calculations at the table.

However, here are some hints that should help you determine whether a check-raise is correct. First, look at the texture of the board. If the river card is likely to give someone a second-best hand that he might believe is the best hand, be more inclined to check. An example is when an ace hits on the end after you have flopped a set, and from the way the hand has been played, you think your opponent called on both the flop and the turn with two overcards.

Second, consider your opponent. Is he the type of player who would always try to pick up the pot if you check, but would not be likely to call with a weak hand if you bet?

Third, consider whether your opponent is afraid of being check-raised. If he is, then checking to him may be a mistake. Many players have this characteristic, especially if even a mildly scary card hits.

And fourth, consider your previous play in the game. Specifically, if you have done some check-raising, be more inclined to bet out. On the other hand, if you have not been check-raising, now may be the time to try it. Remember, in hold 'em, it is important to mix up your play a bit in order to throw your opponents off. However, as we previously have stated, don't mix up your play too much. You only have to do it occasionally to achieve the desired effect.

As far as a check-raise bluff is concerned, it normally will work only against rare opponents in rare situations. Even against good players, it is usually better to come right out betting than to try for a check-raise bluff. The one good time to consider the play is when you have checked a mediocre hand in the hopes of winning a showdown. If your opponent now bets with a hand that you think is only slightly better than yours, a check-raise bluff may be a profitable play.

Here's an example. Suppose you start with

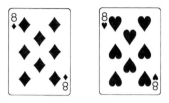

and the flop comes

Notice that your holding is now mediocre, as the flop contains an ace. You bet on both the flop and the turn and are called by an obvious-playing opponent, which makes you think he has an ace but is afraid of his kicker. You also think that if you bet on the river, your opponent will call with his ace. Therefore, you should not bet. But if your opponent bets, he might be susceptible to a check-raise bluff. This doesn't mean that you should go ahead and raise, but this is definitely one of those times that you should *consider* doing so.

When is it the best strategy to check and call? It is when your opponent will bet with any of the hands that he will call with, plus with some hands that are worse (usually bluffs).

An example of this is against an aggressive opponent who has been just calling after two suited cards appeared on the flop, and you are betting top pair on the flop and fourth street. This opponent may have either middle pair, or a flush draw. (Your opponent may not have raised with the flush draw because he figured that you were likely to reraise if you did indeed have a legitimate hand.) If your opponent is on a flush draw and the flush card does not get there, he might attempt to bluff if you check. In addition, an aggressive player often will bet middle pair for value. Consequently, in this situation, a check is frequently correct regardless of the last card.

A check in this spot also will eliminate the possibility of a raise. This is especially beneficial when your opponent has middle pair and the last card, which appears to be a blank, may have given him two pair. When this is the case, he often will raise if you bet, especially if the board is not too threatening.

However, against an opponent who will call your bet more often than he will bet himself, you should bet. This is correct even if you are an underdog when he calls, as long as you were going to call his bet anyway, or when folding would be a close decision if you check and he bets. In the previous example, you would bet if, instead of an aggressive opponent, you were up against someone who was fairly timid and would not bet middle pair but would call with this hand. By the way, in this situation it may appear as though the 55 percent rule has been violated, *but that rule applies only when you are second to act and your opponent has already checked.*

Here's another example. Suppose you have:

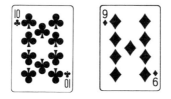

and when all the cards are out, the board is

Notice that when you bet, you could lose to a ten with a better kicker, a flush, or even a full house. However, by betting, you will cause some timid players to call with a queen or an overpair, which they probably would not have bet. (A bad player may also call with even worse hands.) So it is better to bet here, even if you think you are a slight underdog if you are called, rather than to check and call as an even bigger underdog.

Finally, you should check and fold when you are a definite underdog, think a bluff would be unprofitable, and do not think the probability that your opponent is bluffing warrants a call. These situations come up all the time. An example is when you have middle pair and have not improved. Against an opponent who hardly ever bluffs and normally would not bet anything less than top pair, you should fold.

# Strategic Concepts

# Afterthought

Armed with the ideas we already have covered — not to mention those still to come — along with a fair amount of playing experience against reasonable competition, you should be well on your way to becoming an expert hold 'em player. But keep in mind that to be successful at poker you must maintain a great deal of discipline. This is difficult at times, especially in Texas hold 'em.

Also be forewarned that the very knowledge you have acquired could be your downfall. Too often players apply sophisticated plays at the wrong times, and it even seems as though some hold 'em players try sophisticated strategies, and play too many hands, just to impress their opponents. Needless to say, this is not winning poker, no matter what the game. But the penalty can be especially high in hold 'em, since your chance of drawing out on your opponents are not as great as they are in many other forms of poker. Do not allow yourself to fall into this trap.

Also remember that no matter how well you play, you will have some losing nights. (See *Gambling Theory and Other Topics* by Mason Malmuth for an explanation of how often to expect those losses.) However, if you begin to play poorly, either by losing your discipline or by trying lots of sophisticated plays when it is incorrect to do so, you will have a lot more.

# Part Three

# Miscellaneous Topics

# Miscellaneous Topics

# Introduction

So far, we have discussed a lot of different ideas. Yet in hold 'em, an almost infinite number of unique situations and possibilities can occur. Consequently, it is now time to address some of these miscellaneous topics, plus to clarify many of the concepts and ideas that already have been covered.

As you will see, there is much more to winning in this very complex game. This can be partly attributed to the large number of alternate strategies for which a good case can be made. In addition, the fact that so many cards are shared by all the players who participate in a pot makes hold 'em very different from other forms of poker.

Some of the foregoing ideas have never before been correctly discussed in print. This is also true of much of the information that follows. In fact, a great deal of the following material is still not grasped by a large percentage of so-called professional players. Many of these concepts are not easy to comprehend, but once you master them you can consider yourself an expert player — provided that you acquire the experience that is so necessary in achieving success in Texas hold 'em.

Keep in mind that many of the following concepts interact with some of the other concepts and ideas previously discussed. Sometimes an idea will seem to contradict something that was said earlier. However, one of the keys to successful hold 'em play is the ability to balance ideas and to choose the strategy that is best for each situation. Developing the skills that enable you to make these types of decisions does not come easy. In time, however, such expertise can be achieved.

# Being Beat on the River

How do you know when someone absolutely has you beat on the river and you should throw your hand away? Unfortunately, you are never likely to know for sure when you are heads-up. But this is not true for multiway pots. Suppose the flop is

and you have

There is a bet, you raise, and someone cold calls behind you. The turn card is a blank. Again there is a bet, you raise, and the same player cold calls. If the flush card comes on the end, it is now almost impossible for you to have the best hand. Though you can't say for sure that someone has a flush, if he doesn't, then he has you beat already. (Unless of course you are playing against total maniacs.)

Another time you can be fairly sure that a flush card will beat you even when there haven't been raises is when you are in a pot where many players have stayed on the flop, and there are no drawing opportunities other than two flush cards. Perhaps the flop came:

If a flush card appears, you are most likely beaten. It would be different if the flop came:

Now your opponents may be in there on straight draws, and it might be correct to pay off a bet if a spade hits the board.

Perhaps the easiest time to put a player on a flush draw occurs when someone raises on the flop, especially against two or three people, then checks on fourth street after everyone else checks (when a non-flush card hits), but bets on the river if the flush card comes. Folding in this spot is usually correct against typical opponents.

A somewhat related play that most people miss (even those who play for a living) is to bet into possible flush draws on fourth street when you are not sure whether you or your opponent has the better hand.

Here is an example. Suppose you flop top pair but don't have a very good kicker. Perhaps you flopped jacks and also hold a queen. Further suppose there were two suited cards on the flop, and when you bet, your opponent raised.

This raise creates a problem for you. First, recognize that you can easily be beat. Your opponent could hold top pair with a better kicker, an overpair, two pair, or a set. (The action before the flop should give an indication of what he might have.) However, your opponent also may be on a flush draw and is simply trying for a free card. In this situation, the correct play is to just call and see what the turn brings. If a flush card hits, it is now likely that you are beat, and you usually should check and fold.[6] However, if a flush card does not hit, you may very well have the best hand and you do not want to give any free cards. Consequently, you should bet into your opponent again. (If you are raised again, usually fold. It is a rare player who would semi-bluff raise twice in a row.)

---

[6] Against good players, the better play may be to come right out betting when the flush card appears. By doing this, you may get a better one-pair hand to fold. Furthermore, if you still have the best hand, you avoid getting bluffed out, as you probably would be if you check. If you get raised when you make this play, you generally should fold.

# More on the Semi-Bluff

If you semi-bluff on the flop and are called, should you continue betting on fourth street? This depends on the situation. If you bet on the flop, a lot of players will call (perhaps with as little as one overcard) and then routinely throw their hands away for the next bet. This fact argues for betting again. However, if you always bet again, many of your opponents will pick up this pattern and will call or even raise you on fourth street. Consequently, you should give up on many of your semi-bluffs once the turn comes.

Another thing to keep in mind about semi-bluffing is that you should play in such a manner that anyone who tries to keep you honest will make only a small profit. Being conscious of this will keep you from betting too often in situations where you will merely be giving your money away.

Changing the subject slightly, suppose you flop an open-end straight draw and two flush cards are also on board. Is it correct to bet? Some "authorities" claim that this hand should be thrown away. They argue that you can make your hand and still lose the pot. However, they fail to understand that you can bet as a semi-bluff. You often would bet a small pair with an overcard kicker (especially if your kicker is an ace) that has only five outs if you are called. But when you bet an open-end straight draw in this spot and are called, you have either six or eight outs, depending on whether one of your opponents has a flush draw. Clearly, if it is correct to bet the small pair with the big kicker, it is also correct to bet the straight draw when two suited cards are present. This means that if you are against a small number of opponents, a bet is usually the correct strategy. If both you and a lone opponent check on the turn when a blank hits, indicating that you could be against a flush draw, you may be able to steal the pot if another blank falls on the river. This is especially true if you are known to occasionally check-raise on fourth street.

Here's an example. Suppose you start with

and the flop comes

You usually should bet if no one else has yet bet and you do not have many opponents.

A hand that gives you an inside straight draw with two overcards on the flop can be a strong hand. Notice that if you don't win the pot on the flop with a bet, you still may have as many as ten outs. In addition, if your overcards are high, they alone may be enough to win the pot once all the cards are out. (This can easily happen, as your opponent may be going for the bottom end of the straight.) Thus, play this hand strongly — especially against a small number of opponents — and be inclined to bet it a second time regardless of the fourth-street card.

# Getting a Free Card

A related idea to that just discussed is when a bet on the flop is likely to get a free card. It so happens that against typical players, your bet will buy you this free card most of the time, providing that you are in a late position. That is, if you bet and are called, most players will tend to check to you on fourth street.

However, you must worry about being check-raised, which is more a function of the opponents that you are up against than of the cards that appeared on the flop. In fact, some players are much more likely to check-raise than they are to bet out. Consequently, as we have stressed many times before, get to know your opponents and watch how they play even when you are out of the pot.

# Staying With a Draw

Another idea that some so-called authorities have warned against is playing flush draws when a pair is on board. They argue that the probability of running into a full house is just too high to make this play profitable. Well, it certainly is true that you may run into a full house, but this doesn't mean that your hand can't be played. The main thing to consider is how much money is in the pot. In other words, the pot should be offering you somewhat better odds than if there were no pair showing.

It is also very important to consider which pair and off-card are on the flop. For example, if the flop is

someone already may have flopped a full house. Now you need a lot of money in the pot to continue playing a straight or flush draw. On the other hand, if the flop is

it is unlikely that you are looking at a full house. Rational players, even those who do not play well, generally throw away hands like 92. Thus, not only should you at least call with your flush draw if someone else bets, you should bet it yourself if they don't.

Similarly, what about calling with a straight draw when two flush cards have flopped? Many of the same ideas apply. Basically, since you may run into a flush, you need better than normal pot odds to call. If the pot is very small, it is clearly best to fold. However, folding is not an automatic play, and the pots are large enough most of the time to make a call correct. (Also, as previously noted, your best play may be to bet.)

Now suppose the board pairs on fourth street. Should your drawing hands now be thrown away? The answer is, only rarely. However, you need somewhat better pot odds than normal to continue playing. In addition, consider which card has paired and what the other two cards are. Remember that certain cards will make it more likely that someone has made a full house.

However, if the board pairs on fourth street, someone bets, you are next, and there are several players behind you, you need to be aware that you may be raised if you call. Thus you may be forced to put a lot of money in the pot on a 4-to-1 shot that may not be good if the flush or straight card comes. To continue playing in this spot the pot will again need to offer enough extra money to compensate. (Again, in many of today's games this will still be the case. That is, there will have been enough previous action to make it worthwhile to continue playing. Once again consider the board, exactly which card has paired, and the players that you are against.)

# Playing When There Is No Raise Before the Flop

Suppose there has been no raise before the flop. How should you play from the flop on? In many situations, you actually should play tighter since more possible hands may be out and you are getting smaller pot odds. For example, suppose the flop comes with a small pair. If there was an early-position raiser and a couple of callers, you could be fairly sure that no one has a third card of the appropriate rank. However, this would not necessarily be the case if there was no raise, especially if many players took the flop (or if the raise came after many players had already called). A similar example is when three small cards flop, such as

that possibly could give someone a straight. It is unlikely that an opponent would play a 52 or a 75 if the pot was raised preflop, especially if the raise came from an early position. It becomes something to worry about, however, if there was no raise.

Also consider how *well* your opponents play. As previously discussed, when good players have a big card they frequently raise or fold, depending on their kicker. This means that if there was no raise before the flop and the high card on the flop is a jack or less, it is more likely that someone has made top pair. However, if the high card on the flop is a queen or better, a bluff may be the best play, especially if you are against a small number of opponents. (The exception is when an ace flops and you are against a bad player who automatically will play any ace.) Also, if one (or more)

119

of your opponents is "weak tight" — that is, he will release a hand that the board does not hit — then a bluff is even more appropriate.

# Playing When Two Suited Cards Flop

If a two flush flops, you need to adjust your play from those times when three different suits hit. Basically, you should play your good hands more aggressively since there is a better chance that you will be called. You certainly don't want to give any free cards, especially against several opponents. Also, virtually never slowplay. If you slowplay and a third suited card comes on the turn, even if this card does not beat you, it could give an opponent a draw that, if completed, would win the pot.

If your hand is mediocre but normally worth a bet, it is usually correct to check. The reason for this is that you might run into fancy raises or be outdrawn, even if you currently have the best hand. However, you should bet on fourth street if the flush card does not come and you believe there is a good chance that your hand is still best.

Here's an example. You are in the blind and call a raise in a multiway pot with:

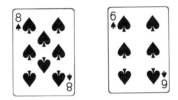

The flop is:

Since the pot is large, you should go for a check-raise to knock out hands like gut shots. (Note: Players with flush draws and open end straight draws will come anyway.) This idea is especially true if the before the flop raiser was in a late position and you think that he will bet automatically. If however, the pot was small so that players with poor draws such as the gut-shot were getting incorrect odds, it might be right to lead on the flop and then try for a check-raise on fourth street.

# Playing When a Pair Flops

Although it's a little-known fact, it is often profitable to bluff when a pair flops, especially if the flop does not include a straight or flush draw.[7]

When making this play you must also keep in mind that a good player will sometimes "play back" at you. That is he will think that it is likely for you to be making this bluff and raise you with a weak hand. When you think that this might be the case, you should consider taking it to a third bet and then betting the rest of the hand. However, don't do this automatically, and remember to consider your opponent.

Sometimes, usually when you have many opponents, you can make a "delayed bluff." If you are in early position, instead of betting immediately when a pair flops, it is often best to check. Now if a good player bets from a late position and you think he is capable of bluffing in this spot, you can call if no one else has entered the pot. Assuming that no one calls behind you, you can bet into your opponent on fourth street. What you have done is mimic a slowplay, and you often will pick up the pot. Notice that it looks as though you called in the hopes of getting some other players between you and the bettor, and you are now afraid that he won't bet if you check. Also notice that if you do get any callers between you and the bettor, your play is essentially ruined.

---

[7]This statement was especially true when *Hold 'em Poker for Advanced Players* was first published in 1988. Today, many more players are aware of this play, but it is still profitable in the right spots.

Here is an example of this play. In a many-handed pot, suppose the flop comes:

You check from an early position, a strong player bets in a late position, you call, and there are no other players. It is now correct to go ahead and bet on the turn, no matter what card hits. Your opponent may even throw a queen away. (This is why you want to be against a strong player when making this bluff.) Keep in mind that many players would never bet on the flop if they held a six. Against such an opponent, this play becomes even better.

# Playing Pairs in the Hole

Incorrectly playing pairs in the hole is a major error that causes many players to lose their money. You must keep in mind that if you do not make trips when an overcard flops — particularly if the overcard is an ace — you are in trouble. This is especially true in a multiway pot.

For example, suppose you have

against four opponents, a king flops, and someone bets into you. If you showed strength before the flop, you are almost always beaten. In addition, you have little chance of improvement. The best play in this spot is usually to throw your hand away. If no one bets and it is checked to you, go ahead and bet. With luck, everyone will fold, or perhaps someone will call with a hand like middle pair.

An exception to this fold is if the bettor is the type of player who will almost always go for a check-raise if he flops a hand as strong as top pair. Now you can't fold, and it may be best to instead raise because he is often on a draw and you need to eliminate the field.

If your pair is JJ, TT, or smaller, it is extremely important to bet into most flops, since there are many overcards that can beat you. However, if an overcard is present on the flop and you are check-raised, you usually should give it up. Occasionally, you might look at the turn card. (This would be one of those loose calls we talked about earlier in the text.) But unless you make a set, you generally should fold on fourth street if your opponent bets.

If an overcard is not present (thus giving you an overpair) and you are raised, you have the option to either reraise or just call (and perhaps raise on a later street). However, after you bet, if there are one or more callers between you and the raiser, then it is very important to make it three bets. By reraising, you are hoping to make the pot a two-person confrontation.

In heads-up situations, you do not automatically discard your hand when an overcard flops. Suppose you have

the flop comes

and your opponent bets. If he is equally likely to bet a ten as a king, then you should of course continue to play. In fact, you might even want to raise, especially if you think there is some chance that your opponent may be betting a draw. However, keep in mind that this is a dangerous play, and to make it, you must know your opponent well.

In addition, you sometimes can semi-bluff with a pair in the hole. Notice that you are not exactly semi-bluffing, since your hand has only a small chance of improvement. You are betting into overcards in the hope of folding out medium pairs.

For example, suppose the flop comes

and you hold

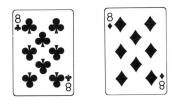

Your bet might cause an opponent with 99, TT, JJ, or QQ to fold — especially if he plays "weak tight." (Even if you don't succeed in getting anyone to fold, it is critical to bet your hand so that players holding overcards to your pair don't get a free card.) Again, if someone else bets or you are check-raised, you usually should fold unless the pot is heads-up and you are against an aggressive player who may be trying to run you off your pair.

Remember that automatically going to the end is a big losing play when you hold pocket pairs in these situations. However, many of your poor-playing opponents automatically will make these calls, and their bad plays will prove profitable for you.

# Playing Trash Hands

Suppose you have a hand like

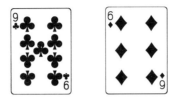

in the big blind and get a free play against three or four opponents. The flop comes:

How should this "trash" hand be played? Is it correct to bet in order to stop free cards from beating you? Or is this a check-and-fold situation?

The answer is: It is a close decision between betting, checking and calling, and checking and folding. If your kicker is good — that is, if it is above a queen — a bet certainly would be correct. But if you do bet, don't bet again unless you improve. If you don't improve, be prepared to throw your hand away on fourth street.

Now suppose the flop is the same as before, but you hold:

How should this hand be played?

Since you can now beat all middle pairs, you should bet on the flop and, if you are not raised, bet again on fourth street. However, if the hand goes to the river, depending upon your opponent and exactly what the board looks like, it may be best to check. In addition, if you are raised on the turn, usually throw the hand away.

Next, suppose the flop is the same as before, but it also includes two suited cards. Now two tens should be played differently. If the pot is short-handed, usually bet. If several players are in, bet only if one of your tens is of the appropriate suit; otherwise, it is best to check. Incidentally, one reason you want to be holding a ten of the appropriate suit is that you don't want to be in the position of making trips when one of your opponents makes a flush.

There is an exception to the above advice. If you are against several players who will play any ace, check and fold any pair below aces if an ace flops, unless the pot odds justify chasing.

# Playing Against a Maniac

In hold 'em, there sometimes will be a "maniac" at your table. A maniac is a person who not only plays much more than his appropriate share of hands, but also constantly raises and reraises, even though the hand he holds does not warrant it. Although the maniac eventually will go broke, he does pose a set of problems for you.

(Note that the best type of opponent is a loose, passive player, as he will call your bets when he shouldn't, and since he rarely bluffs, you almost always know where he stands. That is, you often can safely throw away your hand in spots where you would have to pay off other players, particularly the maniac. In addition, as pointed out earlier in the text, you can successfully play more hands against this type of opponent. Maniacs make it a little tougher to get their money.)

So how do you play against a loose, wild, and extremely aggressive player? If he acts after you do, you must be very selective of the hands you play. Also realize that drawing hands, such as

that require high implied odds go down in value, since you can expect the maniac to raise and thus limit the number of opponents that will see the flop. In other words, you should only play hands made up of high cards and medium or big pairs, unless several people have already called in front of you.

If you act after a maniac, the situation has changed somewhat. This is because when he raises, his standard raising hand is generally much weaker than the average raising hand of a typical opponent. Consequently, if you are going to play against the maniac, be prepared to reraise to punish him for his extra aggressive tendencies. A second benefit of reraising is that you increase your chance of getting the pot heads-up against him.

You usually want to sit to the left of the maniac unless there are some wise players in the game who will not tolerate your strategy and will play or even make it four bets with many hands behind you. But if the other players are going to allow you to reraise him with hands like

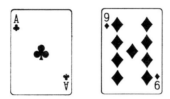

and they still won't try to interfere unless they have a legitimate three bet hand, then you definitely want to be on his left.

If there are other players who will interfere, then it might be best to be on the maniac's right so that you first get a chance to see what they do. Being on his right gives you the opportunity to limp in before the flop or check to him on the later streets. It puts everyone in the middle and then you will have the option to raise. This has many advantages. The only reason to be on his left is to try to isolate him.

Again, if you have a maniac in the game you want to be on his left if the rest of the table will allow you to constantly get him heads-up. If you can't isolate him, you prefer to be on his right because you want to check, and after he bets you can put them in the middle. (If you are heads-up it really doesn't matter since you will almost always check to the maniac if you are first to act.)

So let's assume that a maniac is in your game, he's raising almost every hand, and you are seated to his left. What hands do you play? The answer is that you should play those hands that can win showdowns without improving. This includes hands like A9 and KT, and you'll reraise with them providing that your reraise will almost always get you heads-up. If you do, you should see most of these hands to the end unless it "comes down real bad."

Now you may say that it will be obvious to some of the other players at the table what you are doing. But it still puts them in a bad position when you make it three bets. Unless they are comfortable with trying to interfere with what you are doing — and very few players are — you may be able to play as much as 25 percent of your hands in this fashion provided that you are in a late position and there is no one else (except the maniac) in the pot. If 25 percent seems high, remember the maniac will be playing close to 100 percent of his hands.

# Playing Good Hands When It Is Three Bets Before the Flop

Suppose you have:

You open for two bets, and someone else makes it three bets. How should you play this hand?

Realize that in this situation, you are almost always up against either a big pair, which you may or may not be able to beat, or two high cards, usually AK. This means that if an ace or a king appears on the flop, you generally should check and fold. However, if the flop looks favorable, be prepared to simply check and call all the way. (Occasionally, depending on the board and your opponent, it may be better to bet when all the cards are out.)

There are two reasons for checking and calling. First, if you check-raise and have the worst hand, you will just lose more money. However, if you have the best hand, your opponent may fold on the turn, and you won't win as much money as you could have won.

The second reason for checking and calling is that you encourage your opponent to bluff all the way. Suppose he has:

He may bet this hand not only on the flop, but on the turn and river as well, hoping that you will fold. Give him a chance to throw his money away. Remember, risking free cards is not as dangerous in this spot since you may be beaten anyway.

There is an important exception to only calling before the flop, as opposed to reraising. It is when you believe that your opponent may believe that you might be stealing. This usually occurs when you are first in from a late position, or just by circumstance you have been raising a lot. In this case, if he is somewhat knowledgeable or just very aggressive, he will be quick to make it three bets. Thus you may want to take it to four bets. However, if you only call, you may have him in a very weak position and he may bet on the flop and the turn with very few outs.

For example, if you raise first in with the Q♥Q♠ either one or two positions off the button, an aggressive opponent might make it three bets with a hand like:

Making it four bets is now a viable option. So is playing the hand more aggressively on later streets as well.

Now suppose the flop looks favorable, but you have been three betted while holding

instead of two queens. You still should probably play as before, though your chances have gone down since you may be against tens or jacks. An exception would be when you are against two or three opponents and the reraiser is last to act. Now you may want to come out betting. This might force the players who are between you and the original reraiser to fold, since they will fear another raise.

If you raise with two high cards, get reraised and flop top pair, it is once again usually correct to simply check and call all the way. The obvious exception is of course AK, where you will often raise somewhere along the way. But with other hands you should usually play rather meekly with one pair against someone who has both position on you and has represented a big hand. Discretion is the better part of valor.

# Playing When the Flop
# Is All the Same Suit
## (Or Otherwise Dangerous)

About 5 percent of the time, you can expect to see three cards of the same suit on the flop. This kind of flop creates its own unique problems. Let's see how some different hands should be played.

First, suppose you flop a flush. (This will happen less than 1 percent of the time.) If your flush is small, it is important to bet and/or raise, simply because you do not want to allow a free card that will beat you. Slowplaying this type of hand, as already has been pointed out, is usually a big mistake. If a fourth suited card comes on the turn or the river, depending on the number of opponents you are against, you may have to throw away your flush.

If you flop top pair against a few opponents you generally should bet, as you cannot afford to give a free card, especially if your top pair is not large. However, against a lot of players, it is probably best to check and call as long as you are early to act. If no one yet has a flush it is safe to assume that someone is drawing to it. You should put as little money in the pot as possible until you are fairly sure that you are not against a flush. This, of course, includes seeing that the fourth suited card does not come. Also, if the action behind you is heavy, folding may be your best option. However, you should usually bet if several players have already passed.

If you don't flop top pair but have a high suited card, you should now draw for a flush. However, "high suited card" means one of the top two of that particular suit. Don't call with something like a ten, hoping for a fourth suited card to hit the board. In addition, depending on your opponent(s) and your position, you may want to raise and try for a free card on the turn.

Against a few opponents, a suited flop sometimes will allow you to bluff. As long as your opponents are reasonable players, they won't call your bet on the flop unless they have at least top pair or one of the top two suited cards. And if you are called, you can sometimes successfully bluff through the river.

Finally, if you are against many players, you usually cannot bluff and probably (as just mentioned) should not even bet a hand like top pair. It is better to wait, giving yourself an opportunity to see the action, as well as what card appears on the turn.

By the way, some of the same problems occur when a flop appears with three cards in succession, such as:

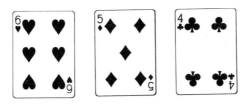

In addition, flops with medium two-card combinations, such as

also pose some of these same problems. It would be a mistake to bluff into several opponents when you see one of these flops. There are just too many ways that a JT or a T9 can hit your opponents, and it becomes almost impossible to steal in these situations. This means that the best way to often play decent hands when one of these combinations appears is to just call on the flop, see what hits on fourth street, and then either fold, call, bet, or raise.

For example, suppose you start with

and the flop is

You should only bet into a small number of players, otherwise, be prepared to check and call.

(An exception would be if you get an opportunity to "thin the field" and you want to do so. For example, if you flop top pair from an early position in a multiway pot, you check, the last player bets, then you should go ahead and check-raise.)

# Important
# Fourth Street Concepts

There are two important concepts that will aid you when playing on fourth street. The first of these is that you should tend to check hands with outs and to bet hands that, if already beaten, have no outs.

For example, suppose you hold

a third suited card comes on fourth street, and neither of your aces is of that suit. Against a typical opponent, the correct play is to bet and then fold if you are raised. Notice that if your opponent does not have a flush, you are not giving him a free card that might beat you. However, if he has a flush, you probably will be raised, and you usually can safely throw away your hand.

The reason you can throw away your hand for a raise is that when you bet, the third suited card on the board will look just as scary to your opponent as it does to you. Consequently, it is unlikely for you to be raised (by a typical player) unless you are now against a completed hand. Notice that this play takes you out of a guessing game. Had you checked, you might have enticed your opponent to bluff, but it would have cost you two bets to keep him honest.

For similar reasons, you should bet an overpair against non-tricky opponents when a smaller pair is on board. Again, if you are raised, you can probably discard your hand. An exception to this (as discussed earlier) is when your overpair is either aces or kings and you think you can induce your opponent to bluff. When you hold either of these high pairs, giving a free card is not as dangerous.

Now suppose that when the third suited card hits on fourth street, you make two pair. In this case you have outs. That is, you can make a full house, which will beat a flush, so this situation is much different. If you bet and are raised you can be fairly sure that you are up against a flush, and you'll wish that you hadn't bet. Consequently, the best play is usually to check and call.

Here's an example. Suppose you start with

and on fourth street the board is

If you are first to act, you generally should check and call.

However, you should not always check two pair on the turn when a third suited card hits. Suppose your opponent checks to you, and you think it is unlikely that he would check a flush because he is afraid that you would fail to bet. In this second case, you should put your chips in the pot. So, if you are against three or more opponents and are first to act, a check is probably the correct play. But if the pot is short-handed, and you are not fearful of the flush, you should strongly consider betting unless you have other reasons to check, especially if the action is checked to you.

You also need to consider, as usual, who you are against. If you are against someone who plays as instructed in this text, it may be wrong to bet and fold when it appears that you have no outs. They may now be raising with a pair and a four-flush so that now you are throwing the best hand away too often. Plus, two aces will frequently make two pair which can beat two smaller pair that you may be up against.

A related strategy occurs when you have two pair or a set on the turn, a third suited card hits, and your opponent bets into you. The correct play usually is to raise. Unless your opponent has the nut flush, the typical player almost always will just call, even if he has a flush. (If he has the nut flush, your opponent might wait until all the cards are out and then try to check-raise.) Now, on the river, if the board pairs and gives you a full house, you should bet after your opponent checks. However, if you do not improve, you should usually check behind him.

Notice that if you hold the worse hand, playing in this fashion will cause you to lose the same amount of money. However, if you improve to a full house, you often gain an extra bet. Another benefit of this play (when you hold two pair) is that your opponent may fold top pair or an overpair and thus cannot draw out on you. (Also, you should play your hand similarly if you hold two aces and one of your aces is of the appropriate suit.)

The second important concept concerning fourth-street play is that you should be betting good hands on the flop, but then frequently check-raising with them on the turn. In fact, this should be routine strategy since you will be giving up on many hands on fourth street. That is, you won't follow through on most of your semi-bluffs and/or the other weak hands that you routinely bet on the flop. Therefore, to avoid giving your hand away, you also must check a lot of good hands. Specifically, when first to act, you probably should check on fourth street as much as 60 percent of the time with your good and bad hands alike, as long as free cards are not a major problem and your opponents are aggressive.

What you are doing is balancing your strategy. Because you are such a threat to check-raise, your more observant opponents will be afraid to bet on the turn after you have checked, thus giving you a free card when you don't have much. Meanwhile, your less observant opponents will be frequently check-raised when you have checked a good hand. By playing this way, you have the best of both worlds.

Here's an example. Suppose you start with

and the flop is

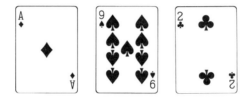

You have bet on the flop, been called, and have every reason to believe that you have the best hand. If a blank hits on fourth street, which means it is still likely that you have the best hand, you frequently should check and be prepared to check-raise if someone else bets.

Another time when you can make this play is when you make a semi-bluff bet into several players when you flop bottom pair with an overcard kicker and the turn gives you three-of-a-kind. You should usually go for a check-raise. On the other hand, if you hit your kicker, especially if it is an ace, you should be more inclined to bet since the ace may scare an opponent who had you beat on the flop, out of betting.

Another advantage to checking a lot of good hands in early position on fourth street is that when you don't have a good hand, depending on the board and what hits on the river, you may be able to steal on the end if both you and your opponent check on the turn. (A word of caution though: Many players are more prone to call your bet if you check on fourth street, as they become suspicious and want to keep you honest.)

There is an exception to the above advice, and that is when the game is very loose. In this situation you won't be making many semi-bluff type bets on the flop, so it won't be as necessary to balance your strategy. But you will still be doing a lot of check-raising anyway, both on the flop and the turn in order to thin out the field. (See "Part Four: Playing in Loose games" which begins on page 151.)

# Other Fourth Street Concepts

Other fourth street concepts worth discussing are detailed below. In the right situations they can add significantly to your profits.

First, it is important *not* to fear cinch hands in most situations. For example, suppose that you have

and flop top two pair with a small card. You bet and get two callers, one before you and one after you. A nine — which could give someone a straight — comes on fourth street, and the first person bets into you. How should you play?

Well, you certainly should not fold. Many typical players, if they actually made a straight, would try for a check-raise. Moreover, this person could easily be betting a hand like jacks and nines or a hand like

which has given him an open end straight draw to go along with his pair. Consequently, your best play is usually to raise. This may cause the player behind you to fold a hand like KQ, which is to your advantage. Notice that a king would give him a better two pair and that a ten would give him a straight.

A play that expert players make against mediocre opposition is to bluff on fourth street from an early position into several opponents, all of whom have checked on the flop. This play works best when the turn card is not an overcard or a third suited card. With little money in the pot your opponents will not want to call with less than top pair, as they will fear you may have been "sandbagging" on the flop. Meanwhile, it is *unlikely* that an opponent will have top pair, since he would have bet it. The expert is getting 2-to-1 or 3-to-1 odds on this play, and it works about half the time as long as the game is not too loose. In some games this play alone can account for a large portion of your ultimate winnings.

Another idea to keep in mind is that some of your opponents are more likely to be weak if they bet the flop, as opposed to check-raising. This is because some players tend to save their better hands for check-raising. So, if you called a bet like this with a weak hand (on the flop), but now pick up something like a flush draw, this may be a good opportunity for a semi-bluff raise as long as you are against someone who you believe is capable of throwing a marginal hand away.

By the way, if you make this raise on fourth street, are called, and do not improve on fifth street, you should usually bet again. Because of the size of the pot your opponent will only need to occasionally fold for this bluff to be correct.

# Desperation Bets

In a previous section we saw that on fourth street proper strategy is to frequently bet hands with no outs and to check hands with outs. A similar play occasionally occurs on the flop, and it is known as a desperation bet.

Sometimes you will be in a situation where there is some chance that you have the best hand and that everyone will fold if you bet. However, if you don't have the best hand, you have little chance of improvement. You should frequently go ahead and bet.

Here's an example. Suppose you call a raise from the big blind with a pair of sixes, are against two opponents, and the flop comes

Notice that you may have the best hand, and that you are getting 6-to-1 from the pot if everyone will fold. You should strongly consider betting. But if you are raised, almost always fold. Even if someone only calls, usually check on the next round. (Against a bad player who would automatically call on the flop with a gut-shot straight draw, but who would now fold on the turn, it might be correct to bet again.)

# Waiting to Raise

Sometimes it is best to wait to the river before you show aggression. This usually occurs when only a small number of players have taken the flop, and you flop a good but not great hand, but one that you still consider to be very strong for the situation. Here's an example, suppose you start with:

You raised before the flop, only the player in the big blind called, and the flop comes:

To your surprise he bets into you. (The reason this is surprising is that with this flop and only one opponent you would automatically bet.) The best strategy is to frequently just call on the flop and fourth street, and then to raise on the river.

So why is this correct? "Conventional wisdom" says to get the raise in right away, and the typical player will do exactly that. But there are good reasons to play the hand as we have described.

First, you need to take into consideration what type of hand your opponent holds. If he is bluffing, he might bet out again in the hope that you will fold. If you raise, he will simply throw his hand away, and you will lose the opportunity to collect more bets from him.

If he is betting middle pair he will have five outs assuming he is not sharing your kicker. By raising, he is likely to call your raise, but will frequently fold on the turn if he does not draw out. Yet by only calling he is likely to bet again on the turn, and check and call on the river. Since the pot is small, you shouldn't object to his staying in with only five outs.

If he has an ace with a weaker kicker, he may easily bet all the way (with only three outs) and you will get him for an extra big bet on the river. But by raising early he might get away from his hand after the flop or revert to a check and call strategy.

And finally, if he has a big hand, such as aces and tens or a set, the strategy of waiting to the river to raise will often save money since an earlier raise would probably result in his reraise.

This brings up an important point. Many players with a good hand, would be quick to reraise you on either the flop or the turn. However, many of these same players will not reraise on the river because they will fear that you slowplayed a "monster."

Similar advice applies when you feel very strongly that your opponent is on a flush draw. Generally, in short-handed situations, it is very difficult to be sure that your opponent is merely on a draw. But occasionally you will run into someone who is quick to bet their draws, but who will check-raise with their best hands (including top pair) and check and call with their mediocre hands. If you know your opponent well, and you feel that this is the case, it is best to wait to fourth street to get the raise in. The idea of raising immediately to get maximum value on the flop is wrong.

If the flush card comes on the turn, you will be happy you didn't raise. However, if a blank comes, your opponent is likely to bet again hoping that you will fold. Since you didn't raise on the flop, he will not give you credit for holding a strong hand and will often feel that one more bet may cause you to fold. Now you can raise and get him for two double size bets when he is a 4-to-1 shot as opposed to two single size bets when he is a 2-to-1 shot.

# Miscellaneous Topics

# Afterthought

We have repeatedly stressed that hold 'em is an extremely complicated game. This is easily seen by the numerous topics discussed in this section alone. In fact, it is probably fair to say that no instructional hold 'em book could cover everything, simply because so many hands are unique to themselves.

Another idea to keep in mind is that you must avoid playing similar hands the same way all the time. Some variation is needed to throw off the better players. However, as we already have pointed out, a lot of deception is not necessary against the weaker players. When this is the case, solid play is usually best. It will get the money.

Also, a lot of the fancier strategies that we have discussed are correct only when the situation and/or conditions are right. Don't fall into the trap of making a lot of great plays just to make great plays. You should be trying to win the most money, not to impress everyone at the table.

This is an important point. Frequently the best players, and this includes us, are accused of being dull unimaginative players. Yet, in many games, this is the best style for getting the money on a consistent basis.

# Part Four

# Playing in Loose Games

# Playing in Loose Games

# Introduction

Since the original edition of this book in 1988, poker has undergone an explosion with hold 'em leading the way. Today there are many new players participating, resulting in much looser games. It is not uncommon, even at the higher limits, to find many players who not only play too many hands, but go too far with their hands. These games, *usually* at the lower limits, are referred to as "no-fold 'em hold 'em."

Needless to say, for the skilled player these games are very profitable. But they do require significant adjustments and many otherwise winning players do not do a good job in this area. In addition, we have yet to see any advice that is totally accurate on how to play in loose games, even though much has been written.

This being the case, we have added an expanded "loose games" section to this twenty-first century edition of *Hold 'em Poker for Advanced Players*. We suggest that you read it many times. It contains some ideas that are quite sophisticated and very different from what you may have previously read. We know that this advice in the appropriate game can be highly profitable.

# An Important Point

Before we delve into strategy, we want to stress a point that is very important in these types of games. When you are playing against bad players, the idea is to make the maximum profit from their mistakes. This is very different from playing perfectly.

For instance, theoretically you could program a computer to play expertly with proper game theory tactics and randomization so that heads-up nobody could beat it. However, that same program would not beat a bad player out of as much as is possible because it would be assuming the other guy is playing well.

Now, there is almost no question that if your opponent plays badly, and you continue to play *assuming* he plays well, you will still win. But you will not win as much as someone who is adjusting to his poor play. And that is why most good players underperform in very good games. They do not adjust enough to optimize the amount of extra profit that can be made when someone is playing badly.

Here's just one example of what we are talking about that doesn't involve specific strategy. When you are against bad players it is probably detrimental to *mull* over your decisions. When you sit there and think, you encourage bad players to play better against you.

You must understand that someone who plays poorly may do so for a variety of reasons. He might be an idiot. He might be drunk. Or he might be there to have fun, and it is not fun to play proper poker. It's too boring — you don't play enough hands.

In many locations you constantly run into people who know how to play pretty well if they have to, but don't. In a tournament they tend to play a little better, but their overall play is poor because they are there to have a good time. Of course they enjoy winning more than losing, but they enjoy playing most of all.

Now suppose that one of these players sees you debating over a decision. Believe it or not, some of them are *unwittingly* turned into better players against you because they begin to realize that there is more to this game than just having fun. We have noticed this over the years, and it usually occurs when a "fun" player sees a guy thinking hard about a particular decision.

So let's say that you are in a game like this, you bet, and someone raises. Decide whether you are going to fold or call *quickly*. Don't give that person, or others at the table, the opportunity to realize that you do in fact *think* about decisions. What may happen if you don't follow this advice is that the "fun" player tightens up against you, but also thinks "You know what, I think I'm going to try to bluff this guy. I don't think I could against someone else, but maybe I'll throw a raise in against him. I don't know if I have the best hand, but he thinks about throwing away so many hands, who knows."

Notice that you accidentally make them play closer to the proper strategy. When a weak player sees you sitting there and thinking, you may cause him to play better, especially against *you*.

If you suffer from this problem, here are some suggestions. Since you only concentrate on hands that are close anyway, you should quickly do one thing or another at random. Since the decision is close, neither one can be that bad. Better yet, every time you would stop to think, just call instead. It's better than thinking.

Another way to get around this problem is to be ready for every situation. Think one step ahead.

An obvious example would be when you flop top pair when there is a two flush on board. If the flush card gets there on the turn and you bet, know ahead of time whether you will call or fold if your opponent raises.

(In a no limit game against experts it is okay to think. They do it all the time. But that is a totally different situation.)

We have a friend who is a very good player, but who exhibits a characteristic that we don't like. When he bets with a good hand he will fold quickly if someone raises him (if he thinks that folding is the correct play). That is good. But he also does the converse, which we disagree with. That is, when he is bluffing and gets raised he thinks for awhile. The reason he does that is that he doesn't want to make it obvious that he is bluffing. So even though he knows that he is never going to call, he still thinks.

Our contention is that against bad players you shouldn't think in this spot either. You shouldn't care whether the guy thought you were bluffing or not. What is more important is that you don't want to portray that you are capable of throwing away good hands for one more bet and that you look at every single decision critically. That can become a disaster when someone unbeknownst to you picks up on it, and steals the pot from you for one extra bet. It is terrible to create an atmosphere where someone whom you have noticed never bluffs will try a bluff only against you. Again, the reason why he tried it against you and not anybody else is the ambiance that you portrayed that has registered in his mind.

You must attempt to display a carefree attitude in your decision making. (However, you don't have to be "everybody's pal" or the "life of the party.") In this way it will be unlikely for the stranger to pick up on you as being one of these guys who "I think I can run a bluff against," thus allowing you to continue to throw your hand away when he does show strength.

Besides stopping bluffs, another reason to act less serious and in an apparently unthinking manner is to keep everyone relaxed and "playing loose." A serious thinking mode of play on your part will not only cause people to make plays against you, but will also often make them tighten up. Players don't want to feel like suckers who are helping this serious pro make a living.

There are other things you should do or not do along these same lines. For instance, you should never make a play that makes a fool of a person. There will be times when a check-raise is clearly your best option. But if it is heads-up and you are against one of these "weakies" who is there for the fun of it — perhaps a tourist — don't do it.

Now we don't pass on this play because we are afraid that it will make him quit. Rather it is because if you make a fool of a guy (with a check-raise for instance in a heads-up spot ), he is going to tighten up against you and focus in on you for the rest of the game. He is no longer there to have fun. He is there to beat you. He is now playing better. You have put him in a frame of mind other than "let's just be here and have a good time."(It is okay to check-raise in multiway pots since no one is likely to take this personally.)

Besides not thinking or acting seriously or using tricky heads-up plays, there are other things you should not do if you want people to play badly. For example, throwing cards or getting mad when you lose a pot. You never want the tourist to say to himself "I'm here to enjoy myself and have comradery with everybody. If I beat this guy he's going to be so upset that it's not going to be fun anymore. I don't want to have to feel guilty when I win."

So these are some non-strategic concepts which are important to know in order to keep bad players playing badly. Badly basically means "weak loose." That is, they are playing too many hands, they are not doing very much bluffing, they are easy to read, and they are going too far with their hands. That's the ultimate for you.

# An Important Concept
## (Borrowed from Razz)

There is an important concept involving loose games and bad players that is best illustrated by a situation in the game of Razz. For those of you who don't know, razz is seven-card stud played for low. The game is explained in detail in the book *Sklansky on Poker.*

One concept that Sklansky addresses, which we will expand on here, is that if you hold a *slightly* better starting hand than your opponent you shouldn't reraise their opening raise if that opponent is a bad player.

Here's why. Suppose you start with a three card 6 and your opponent raises with a seven up indicating a probable three card 7. The problem with reraising him is that when there is a double bet on third street it becomes proper to take a second card on fourth street regardless of what happens. But if there wasn't a double bet on third street, it would be proper to fold on fourth street if you catch a big one and he catches a baby. But, if your opponent is a bad player he will call (on fourth street) regardless of whether there was a reraise or not. In other words, if he has a three card 7 and you have a three card 6, just call him because if he now catches a king and you catch a baby, he'll call you again, even though he shouldn't.

If it comes the other way you will fold and save some money. But if you put a second raise in, fourth street has become a shoot out. You and he will now play the same on fourth street and you will both be correct to take another card off. By putting more money in on third street, you have made the pot so large that you don't give him a chance to make a mistake.

The general idea is that you extract the most money from your opponents by putting them in a position to make big mistakes. Sometimes that means manipulating the pot size into one that is most likely to be a size where they make errors. Occasionally you

157

make the pot bigger early to make them chase more those times you flop a great hand. Other times you keep it smaller to keep the hand from being a "shootout" where you have to chase just like they will. Of course, it is not worth making these plays if you give up too much by doing it. Only in marginal situations should you make a lesser expected value play for the sake of future benefits. But these marginal situations do come up a lot, so try to recognize them.

# Returning to Hold 'em

So, how do you apply the previous concepts to a very good hold 'em game? That is, in a loose, passive game where many people see the flop and then play poorly after that. You should:
1. Play more hands than you would if the players were better, especially if you can get in for a single bet.
2. Frequently keep it to a single bet before the flop more than most people think because you gain a lot when bad players make incorrect calls on the flop and beyond, as long as the pot is kept small.

Lets discuss this in a little more detail. Even if you have a good hand, you should be a little less apt to raise than if you were against better players. This is not only because the hand doesn't play well against many people, but for a second reason: With a hand that is *pretty* good but not great, if you don't raise and thereby cost yourself a *little* bit of money at that point, you gain it back *plus* some because had you made the pot bigger there would be less opportunity for your opponents to make significant mistakes later on.

Here is a general example. Suppose you know that a raise with two particular cards gains you $7 in expectation. It could still be wrong. The problem is that by putting extra money in early you may make your opponent's flop play accidentally correct or close to it. This might cost you more than the small amount gained preflop. Thus while you should play more hands than almost all pros do, a lot of the hands that seem like automatic raises should not be raised because you want your skill to mean more on further rounds.

There is a bit of a two-edged sword here. If you're playing against extremely terrible opponents, it's hard not to raise with pretty good hands because even though you're costing yourself money on the later streets, your're gaining so much before the flop because your hand is usually so much better than theirs. In other words, if people are coming in with absolutely everything, you have got to raise with an AQ simply because your hand is so much better on average than so many of the other players.

But if these players are just playing a little looser than what they normally should, and then they play meekly and badly, a reason not to raise with many of these hands is that when you make the pot larger, you are now making some of your opponents play correctly. This is in addition to the fact that some of these hands, such as the AQ just mentioned, don't play well in multiway pots.

Finally, there is also another reason why you want to play a few more hands in these loose, good games: It is the fact that since you're playing a lot of hands, even if these extra hands don't show much long term profit, your opponents will see this, and when you do have a top quality hand they won't throw their hands away as much because they are frequently seeing you in the pot.

# Two Examples

Suppose you start with:

You should not raise with this hand in many situations because of a variety of reasons. First, you give your hand away. Second, let's say four people limp in and you are on the button. You should probably not raise. Now let's say the flop comes:

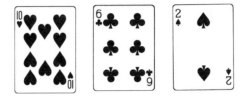

and everyone checks to you. You should bet virtually every time. You likely have the best hand since everyone checked (to a non-raiser), and probably have six outs if you don't.

And by not raising you are more likely to have someone bet into you, and if you do flop an ace or a queen you can raise and force people out who would otherwise have called, getting their price.

One of the problems with raising with this hand is that everyone checks to you on the flop, you bet (assuming you make a pair), and they are getting the proper price to call you with middle or bottom pair (assuming they have a different kicker). So they are no longer making a mistake on the flop when they call.

In general you should not raise with offsuit hands (other than AK), except if you have a chance to isolate a weak opponent. That is, you think you can knock out the players behind you and (hopefully) the blinds. Once you know you can't knock people out, it is often better to just call.

(We are talking about how these hands should be played in a weak game. In a tough game you might wind up playing it the same way but for different reasons. Now the problem with AQ is that it is not that much better than your opponents' hands. So it also may not be right to raise with AQ for a different reason, though a raise would knock people out.)

In poker, there are a lot of hands that when a player on your right bets and you know you can knock people out, you should raise. But if you know that you can't, now you should just call and maybe even fold.

For instance, in a weak game where many players are playing too many hands and going too far with their hands, if the player under the gun limps in and you have

and there are several players still to act behind you, you should fold. In fact, even if you were the player under the gun you should probably fold.

However, on the other side of the coin, if you are against people who play badly, there is not a lot of raising before the flop, and because of the fact of the way these hands materialize, you should play a lot of hands, especially suited hands.

For example, if four people come in, you should play

You do this because:
1. Four people have come in.
2. There was no raise.
3. They play badly.
4. You are going to play it well.

That means if you play K♦5♦, four people come in, you're to the right of the button, and the flop comes:

The first guy bets, and someone calls, you fold. You use your skills to keep yourself from getting trapped.

One of the reasons not to play K♦5♦ is that it can be a problem if a king flops. In other words you can be trapped with this hand. But, if you are a good player, you won't get trapped. You should be able to play K♦5♦, flop a king, and still often fold.

If the flop comes

you are going to have to get involved. Likewise if the flop comes

and everyone checks to you. But there are many cases where you would get away from the second flop.

On the other hand, if you are playing against bad players who will call with any pair, you want to stay in, and you will of course bet it in those situations where it appears that your hand is good. When they call with middle or bottom pair they are almost certainly wrong.

Do you see why we advised earlier in the text to play a hand like Q5s if there is no raise and you are on the button? In the right spot, if you play this hand correctly, it can be profitable. But remember that "correctly" can mean that you hit your hand and still throw it away.

# Looking at Some Odds

Continuing with the concepts of the previous chapter, if someone bets into a multiway pot on the flop and there was a preflop raise you would usually be getting approximately 12-to-1 to call. If there was no preflop raise you would only be getting about 7-to-1. That means that it is often correct strategy to call with bottom pair if there was a raise, but not if there was not a raise. Bad players, however, will make this call no matter what the size of the pot.

Therefore, with a hand like K♦5♦ it makes a big difference if you can get in for no raise. This is because if you flop a king and you get paid by the lower pairs, they are incorrectly paying you. You make money on their calls. So when the game is good, you should play more hands, specifically suited hands, but only if it appears that you can get in cheaply with them.

(The extreme case of this is no limit. If you ever saw a good no limit player against weak players, you will find that he is constantly limping in. He is playing about 1/3 of the hands and limping with almost all of them. He's giving up a little bit before the flop because he can outplay them later.)

The trap that you *don't* want to get into is calling with hands that won't make enough profitable situations. So you throw away a hand like:

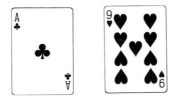

In fact, you frequently should fold AT or KT in these very loose games.

On the other hand, if you are in a loose, passive game where they usually call, but only occasionally raise, you should play any Axs under the gun. You should also be playing a hand like

under the gun, and anything better. You should play these hands because you are going to win a lot when you hit them. That is, you take advantage of bad play. You would also play all pairs. Conversely, you often shouldn't raise with your AK or AQ in spots where you would raise in tougher, tighter games.

# When the Pots Get Big

When the pots get big, this fact should dominate your approach to playing the hand. Large pots create tricky situations from the flop on. Basically your number one priority is to win it. Not to win more money, but to win the pot. However, winning the pot is not that simple. It isn't just a matter of thinking "I have the best hand, therefore I bet." It might be better to check in order to get someone in late position to bet so that you can check-raise. It might be better to bet hoping someone else will raise. And, it might be better to set this up on the previous round.

For instance, suppose you have two kings or two queens in the big blind. The player under the gun raises, and six people call. Our preferred way to play this hand is to not reraise, and then when the flop comes to bet out, unless it includes an ace. You should come out betting enlisting the original preflop raiser to be your unwitting partner to knock people out.

For example, if the flop is

instead of reraising (before the flop) and giving your hand away, and then betting on the flop where most of your opponents will now correctly call you, you should just call (before the flop) and give up a little preflop equity in order to bet on the flop and have the original raiser on your left knock out all those people who were getting the proper price to chase.

It's so important to increase your chance to win the pot that it can be right to bet a hand that you know is beat. For instance, if you have

the flop comes

and the pot is pretty big, it is almost mandatory to bet if you are in early position. You do this not only because you might make a straight, but because it is important to get hands like

 or

out. You would bet even if you knew that someone had a six or a seven in their hand and was going to call you all the way. If a nine or a ten comes on the river you want to maximize your chance of winning. (You should be even more inclined to bet if you have a backdoor flush draw as well.)

This is something that very few players are aware of. In other words, your bet adds some possible ways of winning because when you bet, hands like K♦J♥ and K♠T♣ will fold. The general concept is that if an ace comes and you have the upper end of a gut shot you should usually bet to prevent over cards to your cards from coming, even though they are under cards to the top card, and to fold out someone who shares one of your cards but has a higher kicker.

You must understand that there is a difference between winning a pot 11 percent of the time and 14 percent of the time. This may sound like no big deal, but it can often swing a fold to a play. 11 percent means an 8-to-1 shot. 14 percent means a 6-to-1 shot. Getting back to the above example, what's the chance that a ten or a nine will come in that spot? You have 6 chances twice which is about 25 percent, and if you bet out as we recommend you will win a decent proportion of those times when you make a pair, whereas before it wouldn't have won.

You also have about a 15 percent chance to make your gut shot. So you go from as little as 15 percent to probably over 20 percent because you bet that T9 and knock out these type of hands.

Similar advice applies for a pair (except small pocket pairs). If you are first, the pot is large, and you have a pair, you usually should bet it even if you knew that you were beat. You are not trying to win it right there. If the pot is big enough and you know that you are going to call anyway, you have to bet it. You do this not just because there is a slight chance that you might win if you bet, but also because betting gets out those hands that will cost you the pot a small percentage of the time when your hand improves. Remember, you were going to call anyway.

This means a lot when the pot is big. The point is that when a lot of bets are in the center of the table you don't worry about saving bets. You do everything possible to maximize your chance of winning.

# Another Example

As we have seen, as pots get bigger and bigger, all that matters is doing whatever is necessary to win, and that usually includes a diversity of plays. Sometimes it can get extreme. For instance, if the pot is really large, you might play a hand strangely and seemingly miss bets or raises.

Suppose on the flop the player on your right bets, you have top pair, but you know that if you raise four or five players will come in behind you anyway. If the pot is very big you should just call. Now when the player on your right bets again on fourth street, you can raise and thus force those players who are drawing to beat you, to call two double size bets.

Here's a specific example. You have

you are on the button, and there are seven people in for a triple bet. Now the flop comes:

This may sound insane, but if the player on your right is the first to bet, rather than raise right there, you should often just call and go for the raise on fourth street because *that* raise will knock people out. The raise on the flop won't.

**170**

Now it's true that when you just call on the flop someone will often make two pair. But that's just the point. They were going to call even if you raised and because of the size of the pot they are right to do so. In addition, had you raised and then bet on fourth street, they would call again, and once again be correct.

However, if you play the hand as we suggest, while they can still make two pair to beat you on fourth street, they may not have the opportunity to make two pair on the river. Thus you at least keep them from drawing out on the last card.

Here's another variation of this same play. Suppose you have a pair of aces on the button, many players are in, the pot is very large, the flop comes

and they all check to you. The play is to also check! Then when someone bets on fourth street you raise — unless a ten or a nine comes off.

Again, if someone is going to draw out on you on the turn you can't prevent it anyway. By playing your hand this way you'll be able to stop him from drawing out on you on the end.

The general idea is that these plays may be correct when no one is going to fold for the bet on the flop, but you think that a raise can knock them out on fourth street. But they are not foolproof. The danger is that occasionally someone who would have folded on the flop picks up a backdoor straight or flush draw and now beats you, or maybe he has a small pair in the hole and would have folded, and now makes a set. Another drawback is that you don't collect those on the flop bets when your hand does hold up. But as the pot gets bigger and bigger the pros to these plays usually outweigh the cons.

Just to recap a bit, the most important aspect of these very large pots is to play your hand in such a way that no one will draw out on you on the end. That one edge more than makes up for any missed bets. By sometimes playing in an unorthodox way you can get players out who would have beaten you on the river card because you have managed to cost them two double size bets on the next to the last card. That is worth giving up a lot of other small profits.

# It's Important to be Suited

If your hand is suited in these loose games it is a *giant* advantage. One of the nice things about raising with suited cards before the flop (especially the ace suited), is that when you flop a flush, or for that matter a four-flush, you welcome all bottom pairs calling. They may be right to call, but it doesn't hurt you. They may be making money by calling on the flop because there are other people involved. But they are not taking money from you. They are making you money.

The Fundamental Theorem of Poker states that if somebody is gaining money they are taking it from you.[8] That's true in a heads-up pot, but there are exceptions multiway. For instance, in a four handed pot it could be possible that the fourth player in is gaining $1.00 from the second player in, $1.50 from the third player, but giving $0.75 of it back to you.

So if you flop a four-flush, especially an ace-high four-flush, and a player calls getting 12-to-1 with bottom pair, he may be costing whoever holds top pair money because of the odds that he is getting, and perhaps even costing someone who holds middle pair a little money, but he is not costing you anything. He is rather making you something.

Thus, one of the reasons to raise with these flush cards is because if you flop the draw, by your making the pot bigger, people now play hands that can't win against your hand if you hit it. (This is also why if there are many players in, it is right to raise with small pairs on the button.)

---

[8]See *The Theory of Poker* by David Sklansky.

Let's be specific. Suppose you hold:

If there are five or more people in front of you who have just called, you should raise if you are in a game where the players are fairly weak. However, if they are tough you should just call, and if they are terrible, you should again just call.

When the other players are terrible, there is no reason to make this raise in order to attract their call on the flop because they will stay in anyway. If they are tough, it's not that great a play because they won't play that badly on the flop, and they will have better hands.

When many players have limped in (before the flop), a raise with an A♠8♠ would be a close decision if you were all in at that point. In other words, if you gave yourself an A♠8♠ and you dealt it out against their hands, you probably would break approximately even whether you raised or just called. However, the reason you should sometimes raise is because of how it affects future play. If the raise will get people involved so that if you do flop a four-flush and then complete it you win a giant pot, then that's a valid reason to do it. But if it doesn't achieve this desired effect or if you don't need to build up the pot to get extra calls, then you probably shouldn't do it.

# Playing AQ

Let's look a little closer at AQ (and similar hands). If you hold hands like AQ in early position, you should probably not raise if you are in a game where your raise will fail to cut down the field. In fact, if you are in a good, loose game, you are under the gun, and you choose to only raise with hands like big suited connectors that play well in large multiway pots, there would be nothing wrong with that.

To see why this is correct you must ask yourself when you are in a game like this, "What am I trying to accomplish by raising?"

For your raise with AQ to be correct, you must be able to limit the pot to only a small number of players. If you can't do this, then you must hit the flop to win. You will need to flop an ace or a queen (or some other reasonably good hand) to continue. It would be different if you could limit the field and thus sometimes expect to win with just ace high. But once the game is loose that's usually not the case.

Look at it this way. Suppose you raise with

several players call, but your raise causes another player with the

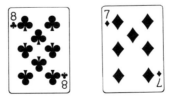

to fold. Are you happy that he folded?

If you were heads-up you might be happy that the 8♣7♦ folded. But once many players are in, you have to flop an ace or a queen, and the 8♣7♦ is only going to hurt you if he catches two of his cards while *you also catch*. Thus he has to hit two out of four cards instead of one out of five so you no longer really want him out.

So if you knew your raise with the A♥Q♠ would force the 8♣7♦ out, but a call will not, that's not a reason for you to raise.

(Of course it would be different if your AQ was suited. Now you should raise for some of the reasons that were discussed previously. A large multiway pot is what you are now aiming for.)

# An Adjustment
# Based on Player's Skill

There is another concept that we want to mention which is very important in good, loose games. Suppose a tough player to your right bets and there is a bad player to your left. If the situation is close between raising and calling, even with the scale normally tipping towards raising, you should not raise. This concept comes up on all betting rounds.

Having the bad player on your left should turn some raises into calls if you think that the raise will knock him out. In other words, on a close decision, be less likely to knock out a bad player behind you, especially if your raise is likely to leave you heads-up with a good player.

This idea is especially obvious on the last betting round. Let's say a good player bets and you have close to the nuts, but not the nuts. It's a mistake to raise him if your raise will shut a player out because the good player may now fold (or reraise). Why not get the call from the weak opponent on your left? You have a better chance than normal for the over call, so go for it.

This concept is generally true on other rounds as well. There are some exceptions where you happen to have the kind of hand that you might want to get heads-up, but in many situations typical players are raising too much and not giving the weak player behind them a chance to call.

If it is extremely important to get heads-up, then definitely try to do it. But if you have a hand that could be played either way, and you are leaning towards raising, if there is a bad player to your left, (and even more so if the original bettor is a good player), just call and keep the bad player in.

There are two reasons for doing this. The obvious one is that when you get to play against a bad player, he's going to make mistakes against you.

There is also a second reason which very few players know to take into account. It has to do with what is known as a protected pot.[9] When you keep a bad player in on a close decision, you won't have to guess as much when a good player bets. He is far less likely to bluff because he knows that even if you fold, the other guy will call. This will have the effect of slowing him down, and you should take advantage of that.

You can sometimes reverse this concept when a bad player is in the hand. Suppose you have

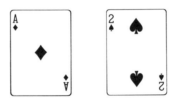

in the big blind, and the flop is

You check, a good player bets, and a bad player calls. You should always go for the check-raise because it will be difficult for the good player to put you on a bluff since you are check-raising not only him, but the bad player as well. And, you both know that the bad player will call you all the way.

By making this check-raise the good player won't try to get fancy with you. Not only will he throw away a middle pair, he might even muck a hand like

---

[9]See *Sklansky on Poker* for more discussion.

and allow you to play the bad player heads-up. And if he does reraise you know you are beat. So by reversing this process you can sometimes take advantage of those times when the good player knows that you're not going to bluff the bad player.

# Playing in Loose Games
# Afterthought

It is true that if you are playing your normal tough game and assume that your opponents are playing well you should still win money in these easy loose games. But you won't win as much as you would if you made some adjustments.

The right strategy to beat loose games is very different than what many people think. The idea is not to immediately punish someone because you happen to have an edge. It is often correct to wait till a later round where your edge might be bigger to make your move. On the other hand, you may discover that your advantage has disappeared and you will be happy that you did not put in those extra bets earlier.

Bad players who play too many hands and go too far with their hands are ideal opponents. But you must make significant adjustments to exploit them to the fullest. This includes what hands you play before the flop, which hands you raise with and which hands you don't, and how you play those hands on the later streets.

It's always important to keep in mind that when the pots become very large the most important aspect to your strategy should be to win them. However, as we pointed out in the text, winning some of these hands is not just a matter of betting. Sometimes, as we have shown, it may be best not to bet at all so that you can try for a raise on the next round.

To conclude this section we want to point out that there is no shortage of loose games. In fact, at the time of this writing, the majority of hold 'em games in cardrooms around the country are of the loose variety. Of course, on average, the small limit games are looser than the higher limit games, and the quality of games does vary with location. But, if you understand the ideas in this section you should be able to exploit these games to the maximum whenever you find yourself sitting with weak players who play too many hands and go too far with them.

# Part Five

# Playing Short-Handed

# Playing Short-Handed

# Introduction

Many players who become reasonably good at hold 'em have trouble when playing short-handed. They discover that their tight but aggressive style doesn't seem to be successful anymore. Furthermore, the "live" players who play too many hands and go too far with their hands all of a sudden seem to be much tougher opponents. Even though they play the same, instead of being easy prey, these live players now seem to be taking down the money.

As we will soon see short-handed play is very different from normal ring game play. Part of the reason for this is that you are forced to play many more hands than you do at a full table. You won't have many players to act behind you, and the flop often doesn't hit anyone.

Short-handed play can also be a lot of fun. At a full table, especially if the game is aggressive, you will have to do a great deal of watching and waiting. This is not the case when playing short-handed. But for those of you who think that the best strategy is to "fire chips with both hands" you will also be surprised. A lot of skill is required to be a winning short-handed player, and this section will show you how it is done.

# What You Must Realize

To be successful at short-handed hold 'em you must realize that if you are not careful an individual could have the best of it by simply always betting. So you must be sure that you do not use a strategy that would be beatable by an opponent betting at every opportunity.

Now it might sound impossible that you can lose against such an opponent. We all know people who play that way get "killed" in a full game. But you need to understand that it is not because of you alone. What foils these wild players is the combination of all the players who keep such a strategy from succeeding. You do contribute to their failing, but only a little bit.

To prove this point let's look at a heads-up game. Suppose just you and another player were playing and you don't adjust after noticing how he is playing. You play your fairly tight game and he has a strategy of always betting. He *must* beat you.

Let's be a little more specific. Let's say he's on the button with the small blind, you have the big blind, and it is a $100-$200 game. That is, there is $50 on the button and you have $100 on the big blind. So to raise he has to put in another $150, and if you don't call he's putting in $150 to win $150.

That means that if you call less than half the time he will show an automatic profit. In fact even if you call a bit more than 50 percent of the time he still will almost certainly profit in these situations since he will not only often steal your blind, but will also sometimes win when you call as well. On the other hand, he is *entitled* to a profit because he has position on you and because you have a larger blind than he does. The idea is to keep his profit to a minimum. This means that when the player on the button raises a lot you must call (or reraise) a lot.

Suppose you only call with the best 33 percent of the hands that you are dealt. Then he can raise every time and if called, be done with it — that is, not bet the flop — unless he flops a good hand. When this is the case, he's going to win $150 two out of three times, plus he's going to win more sometimes. He's going to lose the $150 less than one out of three times.

To stop this simple strategy from working you must develop an appropriate counter strategy, and there are two things that you should do:
1.  Call quite a bit — more than one out of three times.
2.  Reraise frequently.

(Remember we are talking about the case where the game is heads-up and you have the big blind while he has the small blind on the button.)

The second requirement of reraising frequently is very important. You can't allow your opponent to think "When I win, I win $150, and when I lose, I lose $150, and I'm going to win $150 two out of three times." He's got to think that when he loses it will cost him $250, plus future bets.

Notice that we have developed the beginnings of a strategy that should slow him down. Now when you finally get to play that live one heads-up, he won't have the best of you any more.

# The Hands to Call With

Thus it appears that in a heads-up match in the big blind you need to call (or reraise) at least 40 percent of the time against an aggressive opponent. So what hands should you play?

Any pair, is 6 percent; any ace, is about 15 percent; any other two cards that are both nine or higher, is about 12 percent, any other straight flush combination with no gaps or just one gap (except for 42s and 32s), is about 4 percent; and any king little suited that's not already covered, is about 2 percent. This comes to approximately 39 percent. That's basically what we are talking about. (You might add in a few more hands such as J8s, 98, or 97.)

(We do want to caution you about playing hands that contain a deuce or a trey. The trouble with these cards is that if you flop a pair and your hand is best at that moment, virtually any card that comes can beat you. In addition, if you flop nothing and your opponent flops a pair, you frequently find yourself bluffing or calling with only three outs.[10] This doesn't mean that you can't play a hand if it contains a deuce or a trey. But beware that it has some additional problems and these hands may not be as good as they appear.)

---

[10]This little known concept is something that you should consider whether you are first in or not. It also applies to some situations in full games.

# Another Problem

Now we come to a secondary problem. Suppose in our example, you call his raise before the flop, bringing the pot to $400. Furthermore, suppose that on the flop you check and he bets every time. Notice that he is now betting $100 to win $400. So even if you decide to thwart his before the flop plans by frequently calling, it doesn't help you if you screw up from this point on. In fact, (and this is very important), it could backfire on you if you don't carry through properly since he only has to succeed 20 percent of the time to show an automatic profit on his flop bet. That means that if you fold more than 20 percent of the time he again makes money.

So what can you do to prevent this? If you call 40 percent of the time before the flop as we recommend but now try to play "normally," on the flop he's got a *giant* profitable play of betting every single time.

Before analyzing the situation let us look at a similar one. Let's say that you're on the button, you raise before the flop (as you will with a lot of hands), and your opponent calls. Now on the flop he comes out betting every time. What are you going to do?

Notice that if his strategy is to always bet the flop if he calls your raise, and you only call that bet 60 percent of the time he will again be making a very profitable bet. He will be risking $100 to win $400.

In both these situations the proper counter strategy therefore must be to at least call on the flop anytime you have something reasonable, as well as with some other hands that don't appear reasonable. We will address this shortly.

# Calling or Reraising Before the Flop

Before getting into heads-up or short-handed play on the flop, let us get back to other before the flop questions. One is whether to call or reraise out of the big blind when you have decided to play. To answer this you must understand why you reraise in short-handed hold 'em. That is, you do it for future hands, not necessarily for that current hand.

For example, suppose you are in the big blind, you hold

and the player on the button raises, and it is just the two of you. If this was the only hand that you were concerned with, you might be better off calling and trapping your opponent. But poker is a game of many hands, and you need to prevent your adversary from raising with almost anything in this spot. He needs to know that he's in jeopardy of a reraise. Thus you frequently reraise for the sake of future hands, not the hand that you are holding.

If you never were to play another hand in your whole life, you shouldn't raise as much. But against an aggressive player who is going to constantly take advantage of his position to hopefully steal, yet maybe flop something, you must reraise him more than might seem logical.

For example, suppose you are playing $20-$40 and your opponent knows that when you play you frequently charge him an extra bet. Now he can't say to himself "I'm going to put in $40 to try to win $30." Now he will say, "I'm risking $60 to win that $30," because he often reraises.

Of course, he's going to win some of those pots, but still if he knows he's up against a reraiser he's going to be less likely to get too tricky. So in a short-handed game when you are defending out of the big blind you should probably reraise about one out of four times that you play. (In the small blind you would play less hands but reraise a much higher percentage of the time to get out the big blind. See "Part One: The First Two Cards" — "The First Two Cards: Live Blind" on page 40.)

Assuming you reraised, be prepared to do a lot of betting on the flop. You should bet most every time except for your weakest hands, and perhaps your best hands. Good advice might be to check the weakest 20 percent and the best 20 percent of your hands. And, with your best 20 percent, you should usually check-raise on the flop.

Here's an example. If you reraise with

and the flop is

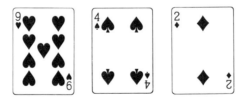

you go ahead and bet. Only check those hands that have almost no chance to win. Bet anything that has a chance.

When trying to decide which hands to just call with and which hands to reraise with in the big blind before the flop, you shouldn't think in terms of precise categories. You should reraise with the very best hands almost every time, and virtually never with the very marginal playing hands. As for the in between hands, you should sometimes reraise and sometimes just call. The J♥T♥ mentioned above would fall in this "sometimes" category. However, if you hold an AK or a big pair, then you should charge your opponent an extra bet almost every time.

# What If It Is Three-Handed ?

We want to pause for a moment and point out that the situation is somewhat different if the pot is three-handed. Suppose in a three way game the player on the button raises. It's true that he better not get away with it more than 50 percent of the time, but if you are in the big blind you don't have the entire responsibility of making sure that he gets called the proper amount. The little blind should also do his share of calling (or reraising).

However, you need to realize that the little blind should be aware that the big blind may also call. Consequently he should only play his better hands. Thus the little blind should play about half as often as the big blind, and their combined playing frequency should be only a little more than it was for the big blind when the game was heads-up. In other words the big blind should play approximately 70 percent as often as before, and the little blind should play approximately 40 percent as often as the big blind played in the previous case.

# Returning to Play
# on the Flop and Beyond

We previously said that you should call on the flop (in the situation just discussed) anytime you have something reasonable and with some other hands that don't appear reasonable. Let's examine this in more detail.

Suppose you call a raise out of the blind with:

This is a proper call.

How often do you flop a hand that under normal circumstances is reasonable? You will flop a pair approximately one third of the time, a straight draw about 8 percent of the time, and you should have two overcards in the neighborhood of 10 percent of the time. That brings us to 50 percent, which is not enough against a very aggressive player who is automatically going to try to steal. Our advice is to *pretend that the top card isn't there!* Take it off the board, or turn it into a deuce in your mind, and see if you would still play. In other words if you have the Q♠T♥ and the flop is

just change it to

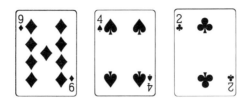

If you do this you should be at approximately the right strategy for playing against super aggressive players who constantly take the pot odds on a steal or a semi-steal. (You would play in this spot since you have two "overcards" and a backdoor straight draw.)

By the way, part of the reason that we have put so much emphasis on this idea is that the strategy of betting every single time is actually pretty close to being the right strategy if you are up against somebody who doesn't realize what is happening to them. You should be playing this way against someone who you think will fall prey to it. If you are up against players who normally play 9 or 10 handed games and don't defend properly, then *you* should be the one taking advantage of the concept that betting every time against a tight player is probably going to show a profit.

However, you don't want to make your strategy completely obvious. Thus you should bet merely most of the time as opposed to every time. Check your truly terrible hands. This way your opponent will less likely figure out that you are stealing all the money.

Another idea that is very important in short-handed play (or in a ring game, for that matter, when you are up against players who play very well) is to throw in a raise with a hand that seems like it is only worth a call. This is because players are doing a lot of semi-bluffing. If they are semi-bluffing, they are hoping that they can win it there or if they don't, they might draw out. You must thwart that strategy, and you can do this by raising with hands that appear to be only calling hands.

Take that Q♠T♥ again. If that is your hand, and the flop is

the right play might be to call your opponent's bet on the flop and then to raise him on fourth street even though your hand only looks like a "pay off" hand. If he's betting a lot of hands on the turn, there is a very good chance that the QT is the best hand, and you need to charge him for making such a play.

Follow this analysis. Suppose you still have that Q♠T♥, a good player bets into you on fourth street, and the board shows:

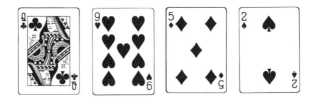

Even if you think that there is a 60 percent chance he has KQ, and a 40 percent chance he has JT you should still raise (or check-raise) even though he will never fold as long as you act after him. You will lose this pot over 60 percent of the time, but if he has KQ and you raise him, he will call and then check to you, and you will check it right behind him. So you lose the same amount as when you don't raise.

But if he has JT, he will most likely call and then check to you. Now you make an extra bet unless he would have bet into you again (as a bluff).

It is true that if you are up against somebody who will always bluff on the river if you only call on the turn, then it doesn't do you any good to raise. But if he will sometimes give up, you must raise to make more money because you make two bets from him every time he misses, as opposed to only those times when he misses and still bets on the end.

On the other hand, if there is a reasonable chance that he might have a reraising hand as well as the JT, then this concept may not apply, then again it still may. Let's say there is a possibility that he has a very strong hand. If he will only reraise you when he does have it that is okay because you fold immediately and lose nothing extra. But if he is a real aggressive player and will reraise with many hands, then you are better off just calling. Against this type of player you save money when he has you beat, and if he does have that lesser hand there's a good chance he'll bet into you on the end anyway, and you'll get the money when he goes ahead and bluffs.

Thus you have to distinguish between players who will "fire the last barrel" when they are semi-bluffing on the turn and players who won't fire the last barrel. If they will fire away, you can afford to flat call them more often. But most of the better short-handed players often give up on the river. They'll bet the flop, bet the turn, but then frequently check it down. And because they play this way, you don't win enough by just calling them on fourth street. These people have to be raised.

# When the
# Blinds are Very Loose

So far we have addressed the idea of how to play when the blinds don't call enough. What if the opposite is true?

Let's say you are on the button with no one else in yet, in a game where the big blind calls 100 percent of the time. In that case you shouldn't raise unless your hand is approximately in the top 40 percent because the blind is going to call, and why put in more money if you are going to get called every time. But there is a play that can be made that you normally never see (except by a "tourist,") yet should be done. It is *just calling on the button.*

When the players in the blinds are very loose or at least highly apt to defend their blinds there are hands that you should just call with. You use this approach when you really don't like your hand that much, and don't want to put any more money in the pot than necessary. (Remember, you are always going to be called.) Yet, your hand is not bad enough to throw away given that you are just against the two blinds.

Three ideal hands to do this with are small pairs such as deuces or treys, small suited connectors, or a hand like:

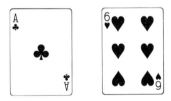

Notice that most people will raise with these. But if you are in a game where both blinds are calling a very high percentage of the time, you should just call. Otherwise you run into problems.

Suppose you raise with the A♣6♥and get two calls. Unless the flop contains an ace your hand is usually not worth much, and you will flop an ace only about one time in five. Though you will also flop a six about one time in five, it might not win, and ace high will win less often still. Thus you probably don't want to commit too much money to the pot before the flop. Another reason to just call before the flop is that you make it more likely that you will steal the pot if they both check on the flop. You should always bet if they do check in this situation.

Thus it is not worth raising with these types of hands unless you have a reasonable chance of stealing the blinds. If you make the chance of stealing the blinds as much as 30 percent, then you should raise with it every time. But if you don't think you can steal the blinds, the play is probably going to hurt you more than it helps. This is especially true if they play reasonably well on the flop and beyond. This is because they will make some semi-bluff type bets where you can't keep them honest.

For example, suppose you raise with A2, or 33, get two calls and it comes:

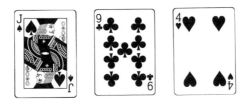

Someone may well bet with hands like KT, QT, T8, or T7, and you will have to fold the best hand. Thus your hand has a lower winning percentage than it appears. So you should often consider just calling on the button.

If, however, you are *one off* the button you should not usually make this play. Now you fold the A♣6♥ (unless you think that there is a reasonable chance that all remaining players will not call enough, in which case you raise). One hand that might be okay to call with is something like 98s. It is probably worth playing cheaply against the two blinds and maybe the button, but isn't worth raising with when there is no chance to steal the pot.

# Leading on the Flop

In a regular ring game when first to act in a two- or three-handed pot the proper strategy is to check many of your hands on the flop. There are many reasons to do this as we have already mentioned, with the simplest reason being that at least one of your opponents is likely to have something worth betting. But this is less likely to be the case in short-handed games.

Thus you frequently come out betting with nothing at all and try to win whenever your opponent doesn't have anything. You usually are getting 4½-to-1 odds on this play. The problem with this bet, however, is that it might look suspicious that you didn't check to the raiser, who will often bet automatically. Most players, if they have a good hand, would have gone for a check-raise.

But it is highly beneficial to be able to bet out and sometimes pick up the pot. So you must be able to preserve this highly profitable play. You can do this by not automatically checking to the raiser when you have something. In other words, in order to make this highly profitable bluff or semi-bluff not look suspicious, you will need to bet into your opponent when you have legitimate hands as well.

In our experience, many of the better short-handed players use this strategy. They call a raise from the blind, and on the flop they frequently bet, and very often they have a legitimate hand.

Now when we say bet your legitimate hands this roughly translates into betting anytime you have a pair or a draw. Heads-up this includes bottom pair because your opponent will frequently have no pair, and he might even throw away some pairs. For example, suppose your opponent raised on the button with a pair of fives and the flop is:

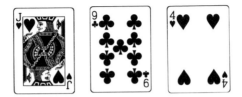

It will be very difficult for him to call if you bet.

So if you often bet out with your decent hands it allows you to also steal when he has nothing. Of course you don't always bet good hands, nor should you bluff too much. But you should balance your bluffs with legitimate bets.

One reason to bet slightly mediocre hands rather than check-raise is that a check-raise puts too much money in the pot and may get your opponent psychologically involved in the hand. He will often call your raise with little and you won't have a good read on his hand. You won't know whether he's slowplaying or just calling all the way with a better hand. The mere fact that he calls when you check-raise on the flop doesn't necessarily suggest that you might not be able to win it with a bet on fourth street. But it does make the play of your hand much more expensive. So one extra advantage of leading is that it increases your chance of winning right on the flop.

By no means are we saying that you should never check-raise the flop. If your strategy was to never check-raise, your opponent would begin to realize that when you do check you don't have anything. Thus, balance is the key. Don't check to the raiser every time you have a legitimate hand, but don't bet out every time either.

To recap, in short-handed games, if you call a raise out of the blind it is important to come out betting far more than in a standard ring game. This is because it is less likely that your opponent has a good hand. Furthermore, you should almost ignore the fact that there was a raise. Sometimes bluff, sometimes bet a mediocre hand,

and sometimes bet a good hand right out. Don't think about the fact that your opponent was the raiser. If this is an aggressive player who will be raising with a lot of hands, automatically checking to him gives him too big an edge.

# Calling on Fourth Street

Let's get back to how often you must call to keep very aggressive players from having an automatic edge on you. The question now becomes, how often do you need to call on fourth street? And, should you still turn that top card into a "deuce" as you did on the flop?

To answer these questions there are three things that you need to realize:

1.  Since the betting limit doubles, your opponent's bet on fourth street is getting poorer odds. In our example he would now be betting $200 to win $600 as compared to $100 to win $400 on the flop.
2.  There is only one card to come. Thus, if you make something, you will only have one street to win more bets, as opposed to two.
3.  Most opponents won't bet as often. Not only does it cost more, but because you called him on the flop he will be afraid that you will call again. There are a lot of players who will automatically raise before the flop, automatically bet on the flop, but then give up on fourth street when they have nothing.

The conclusion is that against all but the wildest players you don't have to call as much as on the flop. However, this does not mean that you revert to a tight strategy. When your opponent bets on fourth street you will still have to do a fair amount of calling since he is usually getting about 3-to-1 from the pot. It's just that you don't need to call quite as frequently as you did on the flop.

Here's an example. The player on the button raises and you call out of the blind with:

The flop comes:

Your opponent bets and you call. The fourth street card is the:

You check, and your opponent again bets. If this is a player who will not automatically bet again on fourth street, you should fold. Your call on the flop will scare many typical players into thinking that you have a calling hand.

# Slowplaying on the Flop

When you are last to act and you are against an extremely aggressive player you should slowplay some hands that don't seem to merit this strategy. For example, suppose you start with

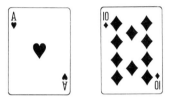

and the flop is

two people check, you are last to act, and one of your opponents is an extremely aggressive player. You should always check, whether you raised or just called preflop, because no matter what comes off, the extremely aggressive player will bet it on fourth street. Furthermore, with a pair of aces there is no overcard that can come to give an opponent a higher pair.[11]

What if the top card was not an ace? Should you still make this play? The answer is that it depends on how aggressive your

---

[11]We want to emphasize that for this play to be correct against two players the extremely aggressive player must be just that — extremely aggressive. However, against one player the requirement of "extremely" aggressive is not totally necessary.

opponent is. If he is super aggressive, it might even be right to check your hand if the flop was

and you have

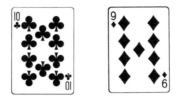

Of course the lower the hand, the less likely this tricky play is worth it. That is because there are more ways to be outdrawn by a hand you could have knocked out on the flop. Still, against super aggressive players you should often check any top pair on the flop. The less aggressive your opponent is, the higher the card needs to be. Judgment coupled with experience will help you perceive when the time is right to check a questionable pair.

In hold 'em, hands come up relatively often where you don't know whether you have the best hand or not, but you *do* know that *if* you have the worst hand you will probably finish with the worst hand, and if you have the best hand you will probably finish with the best hand. These are the clearest cases to slowplay. Everyone thinks that you should slowplay the great hands. But in hold 'em it's not how good your hand is that's important, but how likely slowplaying can cost you the pot.

Therefore the hands that you slowplay are those hands that are most likely to retain their *relative* value in relation to the other possible hands. You don't have to have a great hand to be in that situation. A simple example would be when you hold two kings, and an ace with nothing else flops. You might be beat already, but not betting will only rarely make a difference. On the other hand, if you held two tens in the same situation, slowplaying can be expensive. A king, queen, or a jack can come on the turn.

However, (and this is very important), no matter how unlikely it is that slowplaying will cost you the pot, it isn't something you do when the pot is big. So in multiway pots you should bet or raise, and do as instructed earlier in the text. You should also be more inclined to bet in a full ring game even if the pot is small. The reason for this is that they are more likely to have legitimate hands to pay you off. But when it is short-handed, and especially if you are against a very aggressive player, it makes sense to slowplay more hands than you normally would.

# Fifth Street

In games like this it often doesn't take that much to win. Therefore you must pay off with a lot of hands. Second pair is not just a bluff catcher, since your opponent will sometimes bet third pair for value. You should too, especially if you are last to act and he has already checked. If you are first, however, it is usually better to try to induce a bluff with these mediocre hands. Of course you must mix up your play. (The general concepts of heads-up play on the end are very intricate and are covered fully in *The Theory of Poker* by David Sklansky.)

# A Note on Tells

In a short-handed game not only are you frequently playing heads-up, but you are constantly playing hands that are not very good. Because of this you will often find yourself in a situation where it is far from obvious what you should do, and it is more likely than normal that you could exhibit a tell. The same holds true for your opponents.

Now the tell could be the way you throw your chips in, or the amount of time that you are thinking about a hand. In a short-handed game it is often likely that you are going to have a hand that you haven't played a thousand times before or thought about a lot. You are going to constantly be in debatable situations. It is those debatable situations where you are most likely to give your hand away by how you act.

However, there will be times when you do want to think about a hand. So how do you keep from giving anything away? You do this by at least sometimes thinking on hands that you don't really need to think about.

This idea is very important in short-handed play. You are going to have more obvious thinking situations, and if your opponents see you thinking only in borderline spots, they will have a big advantage.

Here's a simple example. Suppose your opponent bets on the flop and you are having difficulty deciding whether to call. Finally, after much thought you throw your chips into the pot. An astute player will immediately realize what probably happened. He will recognize that there is a good chance that you won't put in a double size bet on the turn. Thus, even if he was out of line, you have encouraged him to steal the pot from you, and he will be correct to do so.

# Playing Short-Handed

# Afterthought

Most successful hold 'em players learn to play in a style that can be characterized as tight and aggressive. This is sometimes referred to as solid poker. In fact, it is the way that we usually recommend to play, and in most games it is the way that we play. But short-handed poker is very different. The tight players don't stand a chance against the live ones who seem to bet and call with anything. Unless you are able to make the adjustments that we described, you will be another loser in the short-handed games, and will be forced to avoid some of the most lucrative situations in all of poker.

The great advantage of short-handed hold 'em, assuming you play it well, is that you get to play many more hands. Thus, if your decisions are better than your opponents, since you will be making many more of these decisions than normal, you can expect to produce a higher win rate in the short-handed games than you would in a regular ring game. This is particularly true if you are against one or more players who only understands how to play at a full table.

Most of the best hold 'em players will tell you that they would rather play short-handed. This is the reason why. They find it far more profitable and actually enjoy it more than play at a full table.

# Part Six

# Playing in Other Non-Standard Games

# Playing in Other Non-Standard Games

## Introduction

In the last two sections we have covered what can be termed as two non-standard games — loose games and short-handed games. There are also other non-standard forms that we wish to address. This needs to be done because if you play a fair amount of hold 'em it is inevitable that you will occasionally find yourself in one of these games.

First however, let's take a moment to quantify what may be called a "standard game." Defining this more clearly, a standard game is one of standard structure (blinds and bet sizes), which is played moderately tight, and includes perhaps two or three fairly good players. Obviously, this is not always the case. Sometimes the game may be wild; sometimes it may be extremely tight. In addition, someone may voluntarily put up an extra large blind — known as a straddle — so that he can "gamble." Finally, the structure may be "spread limit," where bets can be any amount between (and including) two specified limits.

All of these non-standard games require strategy changes for your play to remain optimal. This doesn't mean that you should disregard everything we have already covered. In fact, the material we have presented so far should be your foundation to winning play, no matter what game you may be playing. Nevertheless there are several additional situations that still must be discussed, and in the chapters that follow, we provide some guidelines to help you in some of these other "non-standard" situations.

212

# Wild Games

We'll now address the question of wild games. Suppose you are in a game where seven people regularly come in for the maximum.[12] What kind of starting hands should you play?

Well, it's a two-edged sword. On one hand, because you have seven opponents you want to have a hand that does well against many players, that of course being the suited hands and the pairs. On the other hand, because the pot is being "capped" you are getting very poor implied odds.

Obviously, if seven people came in for a single bet, a hand like

is very nice. There are two reasons. First, it does well multiway, and second, if you do make your hand someone is there to pay you off, meaning that your implied odds are much higher than 7-to-1.

However, if seven people come in for the maximum, you have very little in the way of implied odds. This means that once you are in a game where the pots are being constantly capped, you want to play hands similar to the hands that you would play if there was no betting from the flop on.

When you are in this type of game you would actually win if you only played aces, kings, queens or AKs. For instance, at the $20-$40 limit it would cost you about $3 per hand if you were

---

[12]This would be four or five bets preflop depending on the rules of the poker rooms. It differs from merely loose games where many players see the flop, but only for one or two bets.

never to enter the pot. Waiting for these hands only would cost you about $180 between plays, but those hands should win that back.

Playing this way is both boring and certainly doesn't guarantee a win for any session. You are going to sit there for hours until you get one of these hands. But this strategy will "get the best of it" because too much money is going into the pot compared to the initial blinds. When all that money is incorrectly put into the center of the table, if you just wait for aces, kings, queens, and AKs you must win. Whether you want to splash around with as little as two tens or AJs is up to you. They will win a little, but they also add to your fluctuations.

Which other hands, if any, you should play is highly questionable. The problem is that if they are playing that way, and if they are putting *pressure* on you after the flop, how are you going to play a hand like two nines?

For example, suppose four people are going crazy for $100 each in a $20-$40 game and you know that they are doing it with almost anything. You probably still should throw the two nines away even though it appears that you have the best hand.

You might show a small profit with them if you play them well. But the situation is, if there are only four people in and they are capping it, and you are sitting there with two nines, you are not getting your odds to hit a set, even including your implied odds. Most of the time there is going to be an overcard. What are you going to do then? Are you going to come in for another $100 on the flop, and then again on the turn?

As we said, you don't have to throw this hand away. If you want to add giant fluctuations to your game you can play those two nines. But they don't play well in that kind of game, and the same is even true for two tens. So a good strategy in this type of game would be to play jacks or better pairs, AKs all the way down to maybe AJs, and AK. If there were more players in, then you could play the two nines because you would now be getting proper odds for your set. However, fold them when you are only against four people.

This strategy may seem too tight because a hand like

can look pretty good when your opponents are constantly capping it on anything. But unless you are on the button you don't have to play them. You should understand that you have the "nuts" if you don't play any of these hands. In games where they are all playing crazy there is nothing wrong with playing tighter than what is theoretically proper. It may reduce your win rate a little, but it will reduce your fluctuations greatly.[13] Furthermore, this style will make it less likely that the live ones will quickly make a big win and quit on you.

We understand playing this tightly can become aggravating when you lose several hands in a row and you have to wait many hours before the chips are pushed to you. But eventually you will win that giant pot and be ahead. We also understand that this is a stupid way of playing poker. It's not very satisfying. But it's profitable. So again, stay away from the two nines type of hand. You'll look down and you'll say, "This is the best hand. These idiots are putting all this money in and I have the best hand." Yet, if you don't flop a set, get stubborn and stay to the end, somebody with a ridiculous hand beats you. The problem is that the pots are so large that they are not making a mistake chasing you all the way down. Their mistake is simply putting in all that money before the flop with hands they shouldn't. You don't make that mistake.

---

[13]Keep in mind of course that this strategy is only for those multiway pots that are likely to get capped. Even wild games sometimes have normal pots. For those you would revert to normal loose game strategy.

# Playing in
# Extremely Tight Games

An extremely tight game can still be profitable, unless the game has no significant ante and/or blinds. The profit comes not so much from stealing blinds before the flop, but rather from stealing on the flop and on fourth street. In a very tight game you almost always should bet against one opponent when you flop little or nothing. When you are against more than one opponent and have nothing, the better play is to check on the flop — especially if you are in early position — and see whether your opponents bet. If they do, you should fold. If they don't, you should try to steal the pot on fourth street, except perhaps if an overcard falls.

Realize that your profits from these extremely tight games come mainly from your bluffs. You can't expect to do much better than break even on your legitimate hands, since your average starting hands will be worse than your opponents' starting hands. (You want to play as many hands as you can in a game like this to give you maximum bluffing opportunities.) One word of warning: If your opponents are tough players, as well as being extremely tight, forget about the game. The strategy given will now fail, as your opponents constantly will trap you into bluffing by checking good hands. Leave that game to the world champions.

# Playing
# Against a Live Straddle

Occasionally when someone decides to "gamble," he will put up what is known as a "live straddle." Specifically, the player just to the left of the big blind will post an additional blind that is double the size of the big blind. For example, in a $10-$20 game, the live straddle would be $20. This play is not recommended. However, some significant strategy changes are required when one of your opponents posts a straddle.

To begin with, notice that it is now virtually impossible to steal the blinds. Consider the $10-$20 game with a straddler. Suppose you bring it in for $30. It is a rare player who would post a $20 blind and then not call for just $10 more. In fact, most players who post a straddle will call for an additional $20, no matter what they hold. (Remember, they came to gamble.)

This means that you should raise only with legitimate raising hands. Semi-steal plays before the flop, which are normally so important to winning hold 'em, will not work in this situation. Moreover, you might not want to make the pot so large that it becomes correct to draw to gut shots, bottom pairs, and so forth. Consequently, it is generally correct to raise less frequently with big pairs and big unsuited cards than it would be if there were no live straddle.

Also be aware that your implied odds will not be as good, since it will cost you more to play compared to what you can expect to win. As a result, you should call with fewer hands. Specifically, throw away hands like

and

unless you are in a late position.

Notice that we have just recommended that you play tighter against a live straddle, even though there is more money in the pot. An example will show that this is correct. Suppose you are playing in a crazy $10-$20 hold 'em game, where there are not only the standard $5 and $10 blinds, but also straddlers of $20, $30, and $40. Clearly, if you played only the "nuts" (or extremely strong hands) in this game when you were not in one of the larger blinds, you would be a winner. This is because of the large overlay that you would be getting when you did enter the pot. However, if you played super tight in a standard game, you would not be in enough pots to show a profit.

# Playing in
# Spread Limit Games

Some of the smaller limit games are structured differently from those that we have been discussing. These are known as spread limit games. Specifically, bets are not fixed at a particular size, and you can bet any amount between certain limits. Two common spread limit games are $1-$4, where any bet or raise can be $1, $2, $3, or $4, and $2-$10, where any bet or raise can be as small as $2, or as large as $10, or any dollar amount in between.

Most of what has been covered already also applies to spread limit games. There are, however, a couple of differences that we would like to mention. First, you often can see the flop cheaply, meaning that your implied odds are much larger than in a game with a standard structure. Consequently, many (weak) drawing hands that you normally would not play become playable in a spread limit game, even from an early position.

On the other hand, if you hold a big pair, you want to get as much money as possible into the pot before the flop. By doing so, you will eliminate the large implied odds that the drawing hands generally can get. (One way of accomplishing this is to bet the minimum in an early position with a premium hand such as AA or KK. Then, if someone else raises after other players have called, you should reraise the maximum.)

The second major difference in a spread limit game is that if you limp in for the minimum before the flop and are raised the maximum, you should throw your hand away if you are not holding a hand that plays well in a short-handed pot. In this situation, the large implied odds that you were expecting to get are now no longer available. Those players who do not release hands in this spot are the consistent losers in spread limit games.

For example, suppose you limp in with

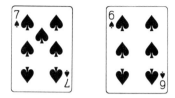

and a player behind you raises the maximum. Unless other players already have called the raise, you should muck your hand. Failure to do so will prove costly in the long run.

# Playing in Other Non-Standard Games

# Afterthought

As you can see, information presented in this section is built upon ideas and concepts covered earlier in the book. For instance, when playing in a spread limit game you can play some weak drawing hands up front due to the large implied odds that you expect, as long as there is not much raising.

In addition, there are countless variations of non-standard games that hold 'em has to offer. We have touched on only a small number of them. However, as just pointed out, the general ideas presented in this section, as well as the previous sections, should enable you to successfully attack almost any form of Texas hold 'em that you may encounter.

# Part Seven

# Other Skills

# Other Skills

# Introduction

There are two additional areas that play a major role in winning at hold 'em (as well as at all forms of poker). They are reading hands and psychology.

Reading hands is both an art and a science. The same is true for correct applications of psychology at the poker table. In both instances, you must know your opponents. More specifically, the better you understand how your opponents think and thus how they play, the better you will be able to choose the correct strategies to use against them.

Even when you are not in a pot, it is still important to pay attention to what is going on. By doing so, you will begin to understand how different opponents play their hands in different situations and what tactics they are most likely to try. Also, you can get a feel for how they think. You will see what they handle easily and what confuses them, and you will get an idea of what strategies work best against them.

Keep in mind that the concepts discussed in this section cannot be mastered quickly. Like many other skills at the hold 'em table, reading hands and applying psychology take a while to learn and require a great deal of experience. But once mastered, they will become significant factors in your winning play. And for those of you who make it to the very big games (against the world champions), you must become an expert in these two areas to have any chance of success.

# Reading Hands

There are three techniques for reading hands in Texas hold 'em. Most commonly, you analyze the meaning of an opponent's check, bet, or raise, and you look at the exposed cards and try to judge from them what his entire hand might be. You then combine the plays he has made *throughout the hand* with the exposed cards and come to a determination about his most likely hand.

In other words, you use logic to read hands. You interpret your opponents' plays on each round and note the cards that appear on the board, paying close attention to the order in which they appear. You then put these two pieces of evidence together — the plays and the cards on the board — to draw a conclusion about an opponent's most likely hand.

Sometimes you can put an opponent on a specific hand quite early. However, in general it's a mistake to do this and then stick to your initial conclusion no matter how things develop. A player who raises before the flop and then raises again when only small cards appear on the flop may have a big pair in the hole, but he also may have just overcards or a draw and is trying for a free card. Drawing a narrow, irreversible conclusion early can lead to costly mistakes later, either because you fold the best hand or because you stay when you shouldn't.

What you should do is to put an opponent on a variety of hands at the start of play, and as play progresses, eliminate some of those hands based on his later play and on the cards that appear on the board. Through this process of elimination, you should have a good idea of what that opponent has (or is drawing to) when the last card is dealt.

Suppose, for instance, that two suited cards appear on the flop and an opponent raises after there has been a bet and a couple of callers, but then checks on the turn when a blank hits. It is now very likely that he is on a flush draw and was buying a free card. If the flush card hits on the end, you usually should fold unless you can beat a flush. If a flush card does not hit, you may want to check and call in hopes that you can induce a bluff. However, if you were also on a flush draw, you may want to bet, since a reasonable chance exists that you can pick up the pot.

At the end of a hand, it becomes especially crucial to have a good idea of what your opponent has. The more accurately you can read hands on the end, the better you can determine your chance of having your opponent beat. This, of course, helps you in deciding how to play your own hand.

In practice, most players at least try to determine whether an opponent has a bad hand, a mediocre hand, a good hand, or a great hand. Let's say your opponent bets on the end. Usually when a person bets, it represents either a bluff, a good hand, or a great hand, but not a mediocre hand. If your opponent had a mediocre hand, he probably would check. If you have only a mediocre hand, you must determine what the chances are that your opponent is bluffing and whether those chances warrant a call in relation to the pot odds.

We have seen that in hold 'em, one way to read hands is to start by considering a variety of possible hands an opponent might have and then to eliminate some of these possibilities as the hand develops. A complementary way to read hands is to work backward. For instance, if the last card is a deuce and an opponent who has just been calling suddenly bets, you think back on his play in earlier rounds. Since it does not seem possible that he would have called this far with only two deuces in the hole, he is either bluffing or has something other than a set of deuces.

Here is another example. Suppose the flop comes:

The first player bets, and the second player raises. A third person, who is also in an early position and is a solid but not overly aggressive player, raises again. Also suppose that several other opponents remain to act behind the reraiser and that this reraiser had just called before the flop. What is his hand?

First, notice that he is not likely to be on a draw trying for a free card since he would not want to shut out the players behind him or the initial bettor. Second, it is easy to rule out a set. The reraiser most likely would have raised before the flop with KK or QQ, but would not play 22 from so early a position. Similarly, it is unlikely that he has AKs, AK, or KQs, as he probably would have raised before the flop with these hands. In addition, he would not make it three bets with a hand like KJs, KJ, KTs, or KT. (It is also doubtful that he would play KJ or KT since they are not suited.) This leaves just one possibility: KQ. If his hand is not suited, he most likely would call with it from an early position, but would still be willing to make it three bets on the flop if he flopped top two pair.

Here's a third example. Before the flop, suppose six people limp in, the pot is then raised by a strong player, and the person on the button cold calls. Everyone else calls. The flop is:

Everyone checks to the button, who bets. Three people call, including the strong player (who raised before the flop). On fourth street comes the:

Everyone checks and the button bets again. There are two callers, including the strong player.

Let's try to figure out the strong player's hand. First, for him to raise so many people before the flop, he must have a hand of value in a multiway pot. Second, for him to call on both the flop and the turn, the pot must be offering him correct odds.

It turns out that there is only one hand that makes sense to be played this way. It is JTs. Because of the high implied odds before the flop, it would be correct to raise with this hand. On the flop, the pot would be large enough to make it correct to call with just a gut shot, and the 9♠ on the turn would produce an open-end straight draw, which would make it correct to call again.

Let us now look at another technique. When you can't actually put a person on a hand, but have reduced his possible holdings to a limited number, you try to use mathematics to determine the chance of his having certain hands rather than others. Then you decide what kind of hand you must have to continue playing.

Sometimes you can use a mathematical procedure based on Bayes' Theorem to determine the chance that an opponent has one hand or another. After deciding on the kinds of hands your opponent would be betting in a particular situation, you determine the probability of your opponent holding each of those hands. Then you compare the probabilities.

Here's an example. Suppose an early-position opponent calls and then reraises. You read him as the type of player who will initially call and then reraise only with AA, KK, AKs, or AK, and you know this is the only way he will play these hands from an early position. The probability that a player will be dealt AA on the first two cards is 0.45 percent. The probability of his getting KK is also 0.45 percent. So he will get AA or KK 0.9 percent of the time on average. The probability that he will be dealt AKs or AK is 1.2 percent. By comparing these two probabilities — 1.2 percent and .9 — percent, you deduce that the chance are 4-to-3 that your opponent does not hold a pair.

Knowing it is slightly more likely that your opponent holds AKs or AK rather than a big pair does not in itself tell you how you should proceed in the play of the hand. Nevertheless, the more you know about the chance of an opponent having one hand rather than another when he bets or raises, the easier it is for you to decide whether to fold, call, or raise.

Here's another example. Suppose you have

the flop comes

and your opponent bets. If you think your opponent is equally likely to bet a ten (probably KT or QT) as an ace, you should at least call. If the turn card is another ace and your opponent bets again, your play is to raise if you know this opponent would still bet if he had only a ten. This is because it is now much more mathematically likely that you have the best hand, and your raise may save you from losing to a fifth-street king or queen. (If reraised, you usually should throw away your hand.)

Finally, as this last example shows, you need to complement mathematical conclusions with what you know about a player. For example, some players almost always will call in an early position with AA, KK, or AKs, but usually will raise with AK offsuit. In this case, if the player calls and then reraises, he is three times more likely to have a pair than AKs.

Another factor in reading hands and deciding how to play your own hand is the number of players in the pot. Any time that someone bets and someone else calls, you are in a much different position than when it is only left up to you to call. In general, a caller ahead of you makes it necessary for you to tighten up significantly, because you no longer have the extra equity that the bettor may be bluffing. Therefore, when your hand is barely worth a call in a heads-up situation, such as when you hold two overcards and are trying to catch a bluff, it is not worth a call when someone else has called ahead of you.

Similar thinking must be employed when you have a minimum or near-minimum raising hand and the player to your right, who has similar standards to yours, raises ahead of you. This means that his hand is probably better than yours, and the correct play is usually to fold.

# Psychology

What we mean by the "psychology of poker" is getting into your opponents' heads, analyzing how they think, figuring out what they think you think, and even determining what they think you think they think. In this sense, the psychology of poker is an extension of reading opponents' hands, and it is also an extension of using deception in the way you play your own hand.

Here is an example. Suppose you have nothing and bluff at a flop that contains a pair. You are raised by a strong opponent who knows you would bluff at this flop. Since you know that he knows you would bluff at this flop, his raise does not mean that he has a good hand. Consequently, because your opponent might also be bluffing, the correct play may be for you to reraise and then to bet again on the turn if necessary.

This brings up another point. The above play works because you are against a strong player whose thinking makes sense. A weak player is a different story. Just as you can't put a weak player on a hand, you can't put him on a thought either. When a pair flops, a weak player might raise (after you bet) with a small pair in his hand, hoping to get a free card that would allow him to draw out on his opponent, who "obviously" has trips.

Very sophisticated hold 'em can go even beyond this third level. For example, suppose two suited cards flop and there is a bet from an early position. A strong player, who thinks his opponent is probably on a flush draw (since this player likes to check-raise a lot when he has a legitimate hand), may now raise with bottom pair and then bet on fourth street. His opponent may realize this and try to check-raise with a flush draw on the turn. The initial raiser now may comprehend this possibility and call his opponent down. When the hand is over, assuming that the flush card does not come, his calls will look fantastic to some opponents, if he actually is against a flush draw. Conversely, if it turns out that the first bettor really has a hand, the calls will look like a "sucker play."

At the expert level of hold 'em, the "skill" of trying to outwit your opponent sometimes can extend to so many levels that your judgment may begin to fail. However, in ordinary play against good players, you should think at least up to the third level. First, think about what your opponent has. Second, think about what your opponent thinks you have. And third, think about what your opponent thinks you think he has. Only when you are playing against weak players, who might not bother to think about what you have and who almost certainly don't think about what you think they have, does it not necessarily pay to go through such thought processes. Against all others, this is crucial to successful play, since deception is a big part of the game.

Several other important ideas play major roles in the psychology of poker. To begin with, when an opponent bets on the end in a situation where he is sure that you are going to call, he is not bluffing. For example, suppose that you bet when all the cards are out and a player raises you. It is rare to find an opponent who is capable of raising on the end as a bluff. Similarly, if you raise when all the cards are out and your opponent reraises, you usually should fold, unless your hand can beat some of the legitimate hands with which he might be raising. (But beware of the player who knows you are capable of these folds.)

However, folding in similar situations is not necessarily correct on fourth street. Tough players will raise on the turn if they hold a mediocre hand that has some potential to become a very strong hand. An example is middle pair on the flop that has now picked up a flush draw. Those of you who automatically fold when raised in these situations are giving up too much. This is especially true at the larger limits, where the games are usually tougher.

A corollary to the principle we are discussing is that if your opponent bets when there appears to be a *good* chance that you will fold, he may *very well* be bluffing. What this means in practice is that if your opponent bets in a situation where he thinks he might be able to get away with a bluff, you have to give more consideration to calling him, even with a mediocre hand.

An example is when no one bets on the flop and a small card hits on the turn. If one of your opponents now bets, and he is the type of player who would try to pick up the pot with nothing, it may be correct to call (or raise) with a relatively weak hand.

In deciding whether to bet, it is equally important to consider what your opponent thinks *you* have. If your opponent suspects a strong hand, you should bluff more. However, you should not bet a fair hand for value in this situation.

An example would be when you reraise before the flop with

three rags come on the flop, and the last card is a king. If you have been betting all the way, it would be difficult for anyone to call on the end with only a small pair.

Conversely, if you know your opponent suspects that you are weak, you should not try to bluff, as you will get caught. But you should bet your fair hands for value.

Varying your play and making an "incorrect" play intentionally are also part of the psychology of hold 'em, because you are trying to affect the thinking of your opponents for future hands. For example, you occasionally can make it three bets before the flop with a hand like:

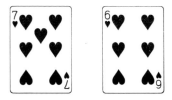

Assuming that your opponents see your hand in a showdown, they should be less inclined to steal against you in a similar situation when rags flop. Also, you are taking advantage of the impression you created to get paid off later when you bet with a legitimate reraising hand.

Another example of this type of play is to throw in an extra raise early in a hand with cards that don't really warrant it, in order to give the *illusion of action*. For instance, you can occasionally raise the pot with a hand like:

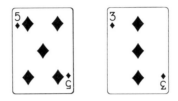

This play costs only a fraction of a bet in mathematical expectation, but gains you a tremendous amount in future action on subsequent hands. However, this play should probably not be made in loose games where you are against people who play too many hands and go too far with their hands, because you get excess action anyway.

There are also other ways to affect your opponents' play on future hands in limit hold 'em. For example, you may want to make what you think is a bad call if you believe this play will keep other players from running over you. If you find that you have been forced to throw away your hand on the end two or three times in a row, you must be prepared to call the next time with a hand that you normally wouldn't call with. This is because you can assume that your opponents have noticed your folding and are apt to try to bluff you.

A less obvious situation where you should think of the future is to sometimes check a good hand in early position on the flop and then check it again on fourth street, even if there was no bet on the flop. Not only may you catch someone stealing on fourth street, but this check also might allow you to steal the pot on fifth street in a future hand when there has been no betting up to that point (especially when an irrelevant card hits the board).

Here's an example. Suppose you are in a blind position in a multiway pot and call a raise before the flop with:

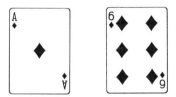

The flop comes:

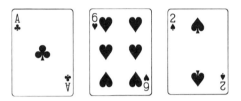

Since giving a free card does not appear to be dangerous, this is the type of hand that you may want to check twice if no one bets. On the surface this is a debatable play. But as just stated, it can work for you both in this hand *and* in future hands, since it sets up future steals on fifth street after checking twice.

In general, you should evaluate any play you make on its merits alone, that is, on its expectation in a given situation. However, you occasionally might want to do something that is theoretically incorrect to create an impression for the future. Once you have opponents thinking one way, you can take advantage of that thinking later.

Finally, keep in mind that these types of plays will work against players who are good enough to try to take advantage of their new-found knowledge, but who are not good enough to realize that you know this, and that they should therefore ignore it. In hold 'em, as in all poker games, there seems to be a large group of players who like to "realize things." You must know how these people think and whether they are thinking only on the level that you are giving them credit for. If they think on a still higher level, you have to step up to that level. (Against really top players who often switch levels you must resort to game theory. See *The Theory of Poker* by David Sklansky.)

# Other Skills

# Afterthought

As you have just seen, reading hands and psychology are extremely important aspects of Texas hold 'em. Put another way, this game is too complex to play by rote. If you always play a certain hand in a certain position a certain way, your game can use a lot of improvement. You must take into account your opponents, how the current hand has been played, how former hands were played, your opponents' perceptions of you, and so on. If you don't consider these factors, you may be able to win, but you never will achieve expert status.

Many of the concepts in this section are most powerful against decent players — that is, players who play in predictable patterns and who are capable of realizing things when at the poker table, especially if they play "weak tight." Against bad players, straightforward play is usually the best approach, and against extremely good players, these ideas probably will only keep you about even with them.

Finally, some players put too much emphasis on the two topics just covered. They are certainly very important, but they are just some of the weapons that the expert has in his hold 'em arsenal. Skill in reading hands and psychology, combined with all the other ideas and concepts that we have addressed, will produce a top player. But as we have stated before, this requires a great deal of thinking about the game and lots of experience playing Texas hold 'em.

# Part Eight

# Questions and Answers

# Questions and Answers

# Introduction

We have covered a great deal of material in this book. However, for many people, reading and learning can be two different things. Consequently, to help you retain some of the more significant ideas, we have reiterated them in a question-and-answer format.

We suggest that after you have read and studied the text, you try to answer the following questions. You probably will want to go over them many times. In addition, we suggest that you cover the answer that immediately follows each question. Only look at the solution after you have answered the question to the best of your ability.

Also, we want to point out that what follows is not a substitute for the text. In fact, some of the ideas in the text are not contained here. But enough material is included so that after you have thoroughly digested the text, the questions should help keep your hold 'em game sharp.

Finally, the questions and answers are organized by topics covered in the text, so you can easily return to the appropriate section for a fuller explanation.

# The First Two Cards:
# Early Position

1. If you are first in, or if there is only a call to your right, what should you be prepared to play?

Those hands in the first four groups.

2. What about a loose game if the players are not too aggressive?

You can add the Group 5 hands, especially the suited connectors.

3. What about a tough game?

Discard the Group 4 hands.

4. What do you do as the game gets more aggressive?

Discard hands such as AJ and KTs.

5. What do we mean when we refer to a loose game?

A game without much before-the-flop raising and with many players in most pots.

6. What do we mean when we say tough game?

A game with a fair amount of raising, but not many large multiway pots.

7. What if you are not sure which type of game you are playing?

Assume that the game is typical until you can determine otherwise.

8. What if the game is loose, but very aggressive?

You should not be in many pots.

9. What if the game is tight, but passive?
   You can play a fair number of hands.

10. Why should you occasionally add a few hands to those you play up front?
    To throw your opponents off.

11. Why would you play a hand like 7♠6♠ up front?
    To stop your more observant opponents from stealing against you when "rags" flop, or if you feel that your early position raises are getting too much respect.

12. What if there is a raise to your right and the game is typical or tough?
    Limit your play to those hands in Groups 1 and 2.

13. What if the game is loose?
    You can play Group 3 as well (beware of AQ).

14. Should you be calling many raises if no one (except the raiser) is in?
    No.

15. What should you be doing?
    Usually folding or occasionally reraising.

16. Against a loose raiser, what additional hands should you play?
    AQ, 99, and 88.

17. Assuming you play against a loose raiser, what do you do?
    Reraise, except just call with AJs and KQs.

18. If no one has yet called, what hands do you almost always raise with?
    AA, KK, QQ, AK, and AQ.

19. What if there have already been callers?
    Usually raise with hands in Group 1 and 2, AQ, and some others at random.

20. What hands do you raise approximately two-thirds of the time?
    AKs, AQs, AJs, and KQs.

21. What if you are against weak opposition?
    Almost always raise with them.

22. What if the game is tight and most players respect your raise?
    Be more inclined to limp with the big suited connectors.

23. When is it correct to limp with AA or KK?
    When your early position raises are not getting any callers.

24. What if you are now raised?
    Frequently, but not always, reraise.

25. What about a hand like T♣9♣ if no one has yet called?
    Raise approximately one-third of the time if the game is typical or tough.

26. What if you are in a game with many weak opponents?
    Just call.

27. What is proper if you call with a large suited connector and are raised?
    Reraise with AKs and possibly AQs.

28. When can you reraise with a hand like J♦T♦?
    If a lot of people are in the pot.

29. What about hands like 8♠7♠?
    If there are a lot of callers, but not much raising, they become playable.

30. What about small pairs?

They can also be played provided that you are sure that you will get a multiway pot. However, they can stand a little more action than the suited connectors.

31. What if the game is moderately aggressive, but features two or more players who will play virtually any ace?

Play A9s, A8s, 77, and 66 as long as the pot is not yet raised.

32. What if no one has opened and you have JJ?

Raise in a tight game and call in a loose game.

33. What if you hold JJ and the pot has been raised and reraised?

Fold.

34. What if you opened with JJ and the pot has been raised and reraised behind you?

Call.

# The First Two Cards: Middle Position

1. Which hands can you play from middle position?
    In an unraised pot you can play all hands in Groups 1-5 when the game is typical or tough. In a loose, passive game it is alright to play Group 6 as well.

2. What if the game is loose-aggressive?
    Throw away weaker hands like K♣J♦ and T♥8♥.

3. What if you are not first in?
    Consider the strength of your opponent. That is, be more inclined to play the marginal hands only against poorer players.

4. What about the small pairs and medium suited connectors if you are first in and the game is loose?
    Throw them away.

5. What if there are already one or more players in and you can anticipate a multiway pot?
    Hands like 2♦2♠ or the 8♣7♣ may become playable if the game conditions are right.

6. What if you are first in with a large suited connector?
    Almost always raise.

7. If you are first in, what hands should you raise with?
    Hands in Groups 1, 2, and 3.

8. What if there have been callers to your right?
    Usually follow the same guidelines.

9. What else should you consider if there are callers to your right and you hold a Group 3 hand?

> How well your opponents play and whether you want a lot of players or a few players.

10. When should you raise with Group 4 hands AJ or KQ?

> When your raise is likely to:
>
> A. Knock out most of the players behind you.
> B. Keep the pot short-handed.
> C. And no strong player has voluntarily entered the pot.

11. What else would you like?

> Tight players in the blinds.

12. What if someone has limped who could hold a dangerous hand?

> Consider folding.

13. If the pot already has been raised, what hands should you reraise with?

> AA, KK, QQ, AKs, and AK, and occasionally other good hands such as T♣9♣ and 8♦8♥.

14. What if the raiser is a loose raiser?

> Use the same guidelines as given for early position play.

15. When should you almost always raise rather than call?

> When:
>
> A. No one has yet entered the pot.
> B. You have a playable hand.
> C. You think there is a reasonable chance that all players behind you will fold.

# The First Two Cards: Late Position

1. How should you play if the pot is short-handed?
   Aggressively unless the blinds and remaining players are loose.

2. What if the pot is already multiway?
   You should be less aggressive unless you hold a hand that plays well in multiway pots.

3. What if you are the first player to enter the pot?
   Any hand that you play is almost always worth a raise.

4. What hands does this usually mean?
   Hands in Groups 1-7.

5. What if there are already callers?
   Raise with Groups 1-3, and sometimes Group 4, and occasionally straight flush combinations from Group 5.

6. What if you hold A♣Q♦ and there are a lot of players in the pot?
   Only call.

7. What if you have 8♥7♥ and several players are already in?
   Then raising is probably a good play.

8. But what if you are against players who not only play too many hands, but also go too far with them?
   Then usually call with 8♥7♥.

9. What is another reason to raise?
   If you think it may buy you the button.

10. When is it correct ro raise with weaker hands in late position?
    When you are against one or two callers who play poorly and did not enter the pot from an early position, and you have a playable hand that would prefer to play against a small number of opponents.

11. Examples?
    A7s, AJ, QJ, and even as weak as QT.

12. What is one of the reasons for making this type of raise?
    Against weak opposition it allows you to "take control" of the pot.

13. What does this mean?
    If your opponents do not flop a hand, a bet will often pick up the pot.

14. What if you choose not to bet?
    Your raise may have gained you a free card.

15. When deciding to make this type of play what else should you consider?
    What your opponent thinks of you.

16. To call a raise cold, what kind of hand is needed?
    A very good hand, even in late position.

17. If several people are already in, even though it has been raised, what other hands can you play?
    Hands like T♦9♦ or 8♣8♠.

18. What about small pairs in this spot?
    You can play if you can anticipate five players.

19. What hands do you reraise with?
    Any Group 1 hand.

20. What if you are against a loose raiser?
    As before, be prepared to reraise with AQ, 99, or 88.

21. When do you almost always reraise with weaker hands?
    When your opponent is first in with a raise from a late position.

22. Should you ever call in this situation?
    It is almost never correct to just call.

23. When would it be right to make the above play with pairs down through sixes and occasionally as weak as fours?
    You need to be against someone who will quickly release on the flop or who will check it down if they have any doubt over their hand.

24. What if you hold a hand like KT, QT, or JT (all offsuit), and a couple of players have called from early or middle position?
    You should often throw it away.

25. When is this particularly true?
    If one of the limpers plays well.

26. What if you are against bad players who will come with many hands?
    They are definitely playable.

27. If you are dead last and there are already callers, what hands can you call with?
    Those in Groups 1-7.

28. What if you have a small pair and are against four or more callers?
    The correct play is to sometimes raise.

29. What does this raise do for you?

It makes the pot larger so that if you hit your hand your opponents may be more inclined to call with just overcards. In addition, they may check to you, giving you a free card.

30. With what other hands is this type of play sometimes correct?

Small suited connectors.

31. If you are on the button and there are many players, what additional hands can you call with if there was no raise?

Those in Group 8 or worse, for example, Q♦5♦.

32. Would you ever make this button call with a hand like 9♣6♦?

No, it is too weak.

33. If no one has called, what can you raise the blind with from last position?

Hands in Groups 1-8.

34. What about a hand like A♦6♣?

You still should raise the blinds if they are either very tight or very weak.

# The First Two Cards:
# Live Blinds

The following questions assume
that you are in one of the blind positions.

1. If no one else has raised, what hands should you raise with from the big blind?
   Only with extremely good hands.

2. Should you raise with very good hands against one or two aggressive opponents who have just called?
   No. Your best play usually is to call.

3. Why is this your best play?
   Because you can try for a check-raise later.

4. Do you have to hit your hand for the check-raise to be correct?
   No, you just need to be fairly sure that the flop did not help anyone.

5. If you hold AK in the big blind and are called by only one or two players in late position, what should you do?
   Raise.

6. When is another time that it is sometimes correct to raise in the big blind?
   When several people have called and you hold a hand like JTs, A5s, or a small pair.

7. If there is a raise to your right, which hands can you call with in the big blind?
   Only with your better hands.

8. What is the problem with calling in this spot?
Someone on your left may reraise.

9. But what if many players are in the pot?
You should play more hands, especially hands that have the potential to make big hands.

10. Should you call a raise out of the big blind with a hand like 5♣4♥?
No.

11. Would it be okay if this hand was suited?
Yes.

12. For these calls to be profitable what do you need?
At least two ways to win.

13. What if your cards were higher?
You might win if you make a pair after the flop.

14. When is it correct to call with a small unsuited connecting hand?
If you are against weak players who will not extract the maximum from you when you flop a draw, but who will frequently pay off if you make something.

15. When the pot is raised early, what type of hands demand special attention?
Hands like AJ, AT, KJ, and KT.

16. Why?
They can easily make second best hands that you will have to pay off all the way.

17. To call with a small pair, how many players do you usually need?
    Two.

18. Usually reraise with?
    AA or KK.

19. What if you are in the big blind and are against a possible steal-raise?
    You can call with hands as weak as those in Group 8.

20. What if someone calls in between you and your opponent, or if your opponent plays well?
    Tighten up some; Groups 1-6.

21. What about when you are in the little blind and are against a possible steal-raise?
    You can play Groups 1-6, but you should almost always reraise.

22. What is the purpose of this reraise?
    To drive the big blind out of the pot.

23. What if someone else has already called the raise?
    This play is usually incorrect.

24. What if the pot is not raised and you are in the little blind?
    If it costs only half a bet to call, still be somewhat selective of the hands you play. If it costs only one-third of a bet, every hand should be played.

25. What is the one exception?
    If the big blind is a frequent raiser. Now you must fold more often.

26. If no one has raised, the pot is short-handed, you are in the small blind, and the big blind is apt to call your raise, what hands should you raise with?

Only your best hands.

27. What if the big blind will fold a lot?

Raise with many more hands.

28. What if no one has raised, the pot is multiway, and you are in the small blind?

Only raise with hands that are either very strong or some hands that play well multiway.

29. What if you are in the small blind, everyone has folded, and the big blind throws away too many hands?

You should frequently raise.

30. An Example?

Everyone has passed and you hold A♥6♦ in the little blind. You should frequently call. However, if the big blind folds a lot, or folds too much on the flop, you should always raise.

31. What if you are in the big blind, everyone passes to the little blind, and he raises. What do you need to do?

You need to call enough so that the player in the little blind does not show an automatic profit.

32. But what if you know that the player in the little blind has high raising standards?

You should fold your weaker hands.

# Semi-Bluffing

1. What is a semi-bluff?

   A bet with a hand which, if called, does not figure to be the best hand at the moment, but has a reasonable chance of outdrawing those hands that initially called it.

2. What are some obvious examples of semi-bluff situations?

   You have flopped an inside straight draw, or second or third pair with an overcard kicker.

3. Cite a specific example?

   You have T♠9♠ against not too many opponents, and the flop comes 7♣6♦2♠.

4. Why might you not want to semi-bluff in last position?

   You may be check-raised.

5. Therefore, what is one of the determining factors about semi-bluffing when you are last?

   How frequently you think you will be check-raised.

6. What else might your semi-bluff bet do for you in last position?

   It might buy you a free card.

7. Give some examples of correct semi-bluff situations?

   A four-flush or an open-end straight draw, especially with a pair, with one card to come; a small pair with an overcard kicker on the flop; and a small gut shot when the flop includes a high card.

8. What is a good rule to follow when determining whether to semi-bluff?

If your hand is either worth a call or almost worth a call if you check, then it is better to bet if there is some chance that you can win the pot right there.

9. What is a secondary advantage to semi-bluffing?

When you make your hand, your opponent often will misread it.

10. What is a third advantage of semi-bluffing?

It keeps your opponents guessing.

11. What happens if you never bluff?

You are giving away too much information when you do bet.

12. What is a fourth advantage of semi-bluffing?

You may get a free card on the next round.

13. When is it correct to bet two overcards?

Frequently, especially if you have backdoor flush potential.

14. What is an exception?

You think a reasonable chance exists that if you catch your card, you still won't win.

15. When would you be less likely to bet two overcards?

When a straight type flop hits, or a flop with two suited cards.

16. If you bet two overcards on the flop and are raised, should you call?

The answer depends on whether you think you will be able to win if one of your overcards hits, and on the pot odds that you are getting.

17. If small cards flop, why should you be more inclined to call with KQ than with AK?

This is because many more people play hands like Ax than Kx.

# The Free Card

1. Should you bet most of your legitimate hands?
   Yes, to give your opponent a chance to drop.

2. Does this include four-flushes and open-end straight draws with two cards to come?
   Yes.

3. Should you bet open-end straight draws if two cards of the same suit flop?
   Yes.

4. Should you bet top pair or an over pair on the flop?
   Yes, if it figures to be the best hand.

5. What are the exceptions?
   When there is a lot of raising before the flop (indicating that you may not have the best hand), and those times when you have decided to check-raise.

6. Should you check to the before-the-flop raiser?
   No. Fight this tendency.

7. What is rarely correct hold 'em strategy?
   Checking and calling.

8. When is checking and calling correct?
   It is correct when:
   A.   You are slowplaying.
   B.   You are fairly sure that your opponent has a better hand and will not fold if you bet, but the pot odds justify your calling in the hope that either you do have the best hand or you may outdraw him.
   C.   You are against a habitual bluffer.

9. Why might giving a free card be incorrect even when you are a big favorite and want callers?

Because the next card might be a miracle for someone, but it is not likely to make anyone a second best hand.

10. Example?

You have flopped a small flush.

11. What is the general principle of free cards?

If you check and allow someone who would not have called your bet to outdraw you, then you have allowed a "mathematical catastrophe" to happen.

12. When is it also a catastrophe (though not as bad)?

When you give a free card to an opponent who would have called your bet, and he fails to outdraw you.

13. Name four other times when it is correct to check on the flop.

This is correct when:

A. You are sure that you don't have the best hand and especially sure that you will be called if you bet.

B. You think it is likely that someone behind you will bet.

C. You have a hand that should be slowplayed.

D. You have flopped top pair, either aces or kings, and you have a weak kicker.

14. When does it often occur that someone will bet behind you?

You are in a two or three person pot and were raised by an aggressive opponent before the flop.

15. Suppose you have flopped top pair, but not aces or kings, and you have a weak kicker. You are in an early position, and the pot was not raised. How should your hand be played?

Against a small number of opponents, you should bet so you are not giving a free card. Against a large number of opponents, you should check and fold if it is bet early, but check-raise if a late position player bets.

16. In this situation, what if your top pair (with a weak kicker) is below queens?

You must be cautious.

17. Why?

It is more probable for someone else to have top pair in an unraised pot when the top card is a jack or lower.

18. If you are the before-the-flop raiser in a multiway pot, your hand is weak, and everyone checks to you, should you take a free card?

Yes, you almost always should take a free card.

19. What if the pot is short-handed?

You should usually bet because there is a reasonable chance you can win the pot right there.

20. Suppose you have A♠K♠, the flop is 7♣6♠2♦, and everyone checks to you. What should you do?

Bet if the pot is short-handed. You don't want to give a free card to someone holding a hand like J♥T♦.

21. Why is betting or raising in late position with a hand that does not seem to justify it sometimes correct?

Because you may gain a free card on the next round.

22. What must you keep in mind if you take that free card?
    Some opponents automatically will bet on the river, no matter what they have or what the last card is.

23. What is a good hand to check the flop after it is checked to you, and then bet the turn if a high card hits?
    AJ. You will have six legitimate cards to bet — your pair cards, and eight cards to bluff with.

24. Is it usually correct to raise in late position on the flop with a four-flush?
    Unless the game is tough, this play is generally correct. You should raise more than half the time.

25. Even if you can't get a free card, how many callers do you need to get sufficient odds on your raise?
    Three.

26. What is an exception to raising?
    If a pair flopped.

27. What should you do any time that you are in late position on the flop and have a hand that is worth a call?
    Seriously consider raising.

28. Even if you are sure that the bettor has you beat, it may be worth a raise. Can you give an example?
    Five players have put in three bets each before the flop. You are in last position with Q♠J♠ and are almost sure that no one has aces or kings since you put in the last raise. The flop is T♠7♦3♥. If the player to your right bets after everyone else has checked, you should raise — even if you are sure that he has two tens.

262 Part Eight: Questions and Answers

29. You have A♥7♥. The flop includes an ace and one of your suit.
How do you play if someone bets?

> Raise and then bet on the turn with the intention of just
> showing down on the river if you do not improve. (If you get
> check-raised on fourth street, you usually should fold, unless
> you helped or picked up a flush draw.)

# Slowplaying

1. What criteria must be met for a slowplay to be correct?
   A.   Your hand must be very strong.
   B.   You probably will chase everyone out by betting, but you have a good chance of winning a large pot if you check.
   C.   The free card that you are giving has good possibilities of making second best hands.
   D.   This free card has little chance of making a better hand or a profitable drawing hand for someone else.
   E.   The pot must not be very large.

2. Give an example of a correct slowplay?
   You have JJ and the flop comes J♣6♥2♦.

3. But what if you have a lot of opponents?
   Slowplaying may not be correct if the pot has become large.

4. If the situation is not perfect, should you slowplay?
   No.

5. Example?
   The flop is Q♠J♠3♣ and you have 3♦3♥. You usually should bet or raise on the flop, as your opponents can hold many possible hands, including flush and straight draws.

6. When is another time that you usually should not slowplay?
   When you have flopped the absolute nuts. This is because an opponent also may have flopped a very strong hand and will give you plenty of action.

7. What is an exception?
   You have all the good cards (e.g. you hold A7 and the flop is A77).

8. What if you hold two aces and a third ace flops?
   It is generally correct to bet. There is usually not a second-best hand for your opponents to make.

9. When would it be right to check in this spot?
   If you think it will entice a bluff.

10. What kind of hand do you need to just call someone else's bet in order to reraise a raiser behind you or to go for a raise on fourth street?
   A hand almost as strong as a regular slowplaying hand.

11. Give an example of this play?
   You flop top two pair, and the player on your immediate right bets into you. You may want to wait until the turn to raise. However, should a third player raise behind you, it is probably better to reraise on the flop and gain extra bets from all of your opponents.

# Check-Raising

1. In limit hold 'em, what is sometimes the best reason to check-raise?

To exclude opponents from competing for the pot.

2. When is it correct to check-raise?
When:
A. You think you have the best hand (though not a slowplaying hand).
B. You are quite sure that someone will bet behind you.

3. Is it ever correct to check-raise with a drawing hand?
This is correct when you think a player to your left will bet and two or more players will call.

4. Is this how a four-flush or an open-end straight draw normally should be played?
No. Normally you should bet if this may enable you to steal the pot.

5. What may happen if you check a lot of good hands on the flop?
Some of your opponents may become afraid to bet. That is, they may be more inclined to give you a free card, and this free card may win the pot for you.

6. But what if this free card is a blank?
You now may be able to steal the pot.

7. What else might happen if you check a lot of hands on the flop?
The free card that you give occasionally may cost you the pot.

8. Can you check-raise semi-bluff?
Yes.

9. Example?
   You have T♦9♦, and the flop is 8♦4♠2♣. You bet and are raised, and you (correctly) call. The next card is the J♦. You should check-raise.

10. Another example?
    You have Q♠J♠, and the flop comes Q♣8♦4♠. If any spade hits on fourth street, you should check-raise.

11. What is another very important reason to check-raise?
    In games of today's structure, the bet on the flop is often not large enough, when compared to the size of the pot, to make it incorrect for drawing hands (and this includes hands like middle pair) to call. This means that you should check-raise a fair amount in an attempt to cut down the odds for opponents to draw out on you when the pot is large.

12. What is a good guideline to follow?
    Consider check-raising if it is unlikely that an overcard can hurt you.

13. Be specific:
    If you flop top pair and your top pair is aces, kings, or queens (and you have an overcard kicker with your queen), check-raising is frequently the correct play.

14. What if it is a large multiway pot, you have top pair, but you are afraid of an overcard?
    It still may be correct to check-raise, especially if you are in an early position.

15. Why?
    This is because the pot is now so large that if you bet, you can expect a lot of callers anyway. Consequently, in an effort to thin the field, it may be necessary to risk the dreaded free card.

6. Example?

You are in early position with Q♣J♣ in a large multiway pot. The flop is J♠7♥2♦. You must consider going for a check-raise.

# Odds and Implied Odds

1. If the bettor is to your right and there are other players who might raise behind you, what must you do?

    Adjust the pot odds considerably lower.

2. What does this mean?

    Fold more hands.

3. Example?

    You hold A♣8♣, and the flop is A♠Q♠9♦. If a solid player to your right bets, a number of players are behind you, and there has been no raise before the flop, you should fold.

4. What if you are against a loose bettor?

    You should raise rather than fold.

5. When else should you continue to play?

    Against a player who will only bet a draw.

6. Another example?

    In the same situation, fold K♦J♦ if the flop is J♠T♠8♥.

7. What are other exceptions to folding these hands?

    If the pot has become very large and/or the game is very loose.

8. How does it affect the pot odds you are getting if you call on the flop and intend to also call on fourth street?

    They are not as good as they appear.

9. When is it correct to call before the flop with a small pair?

    When you are getting as low as 5-to-1 odds and there is little fear of a raise behind you.

10. What if you are against players who give a lot of action?
    You can make this call even if you are getting a bit less than 5-to-1.

11. A second example?
    You can try for an inside straight on the flop when you have odds of only about 8-to-1.

12. Why should you make a loose call every now and then, even if the odds don't seem to justify it?
    Because you don't want to become known as a "folder."

13. What happens if you are regarded as a folder?
    Other players will try to run over you, and otherwise predictable opponents may turn tricky and become difficult to play against.

# Bluffing

1. When should you bluff?
   When you think that the size of the pot, compared to the estimated probability that your opponent will fold, is large enough to make this play profitable (in terms of long run expectation).

2. Why should you sometimes bluff if the odds don't seem to justify it?
   This makes it more difficult for your opponent to read your hands in the future.

3. What is an example of a good fifth-street bluff?
   You have only one opponent remaining, you are trying for a straight, and a third suited card appears on board. Against a player who is capable of folding, you may want to attempt a bluff.

4. What is an example of an obvious fourth-street bluff?
   You are in late position and everyone has checked on both the flop and fourth street.

5. If the top card on board pairs on fourth street, what does this mean if you bet the flop and weren't raised?
   This is a good spot to bet again.

6. What is an example of a good bluffing opportunity on the flop?
   In a short-handed pot, when no one has shown any strength before the flop, if you are in an early position and the flop comes either ace high or king high with no flush or straight draws, a bet should steal it enough to be profitable.

7. What is a specific example?

Flops like K♦8♥3♠ are excellent candidates for this type of bluff.

8. If all the cards are out and your hand can only beat a bluff, what does your decision to call depend on?

Your pot odds and on your judgment concerning the chance that your opponent is bluffing.

9. What if your hand can beat some of the hands he would bet for value, as well as his bluffs?

You do not need as great a price.

# Inducing Bluffs

1. What are you trying to do when you induce a bluff?
   Manipulate your opponent into betting a hand that he originally had no intention of betting.

2. When does making what seems to be an irrational check work best?
   When you are against an aggressive player.

3. What is an example?
   You hold either AA or KK and raise in last position. The flop comes with a medium or small pair. It is checked to you, you bet, and a tough player calls. On fourth street the correct play is often to check behind your opponent if he checks again.

4. What is a similar example?
   You have AA or KK and the top card on board pairs on the turn.

5. Before inducing a bluff, what criteria need to be met?
   A.  A small number of opponents, preferably just one.
   B.  You need to be against a player who is capable of bluffing, but also capable of folding if you bet.
   C.  Giving a free card to your opponent is not dangerous if his hand is worse than yours.

6. Another example?
   You hold A♥4♥ and raise from late position. You are reraised by the player in the big blind, and the flop comes A♣K♦3♠. Your opponent bets and you call. On fourth street, a blank hits and your opponent checks. You also should check with the intention of betting or calling on the river.

272

7. A third example?

You are in late position against several opponents. A fourth suited card hits on the turn, you have the king of that suit, and everyone has checked to you. The correct play may be for you to also check.

# Folding When the Pot is Big

1. What must you be aware of?
   In hold 'em, situations sometimes develop where it is virtually impossible for your opponent to be bluffing.

2. What does this mean?
   Even though the pot may be quite large, it is frequently correct to throw away your hand.

3. Example?
   Suppose the pot is many-handed and you get a free play in the big blind. You hold 7♦2♣ and the flop comes 7♥6♣2♠. You check, planning to check-raise, but no one bets. The fourth street card is the Q♦. Again you check, planning to check-raise. And this time one player does bet, another calls, and you check-raise. On fifth street, another queen hits. You should now check and fold.

# Heads-Up Versus Multiway

1. How do you play with many opponents?
   Less fancy. Slowplay less, semi-bluff less, avoid bluffing, and avoid inducing bluffs with checks that give free cards.

2. What about your implied odds?
   They have increased.

3. What does this mean?
   You should be much more apt to play and even raise with small pairs, suited connectors, and hands like A♠6♠.

4. What else?
   You should not raise with unsuited high cards, and it may be right to fold hands like AT, KT, and even AJ and KJ.

5. Example?
   You hold K♦T♥ on the button, and five or six players have limped in. You should strongly consider folding.

6. What happens on the flop?
   Many hands play differently depending on the size of the pot and the number of players in the pot.

7. Suppose you have A♠K♣, the flop is A♦T♣3♦. If the player on your right bets into you, what should you do?
   If the pot is small you may only want to call. But if the pot is big you would now want to raise.

8. Suppose you flop a small flush draw and the pot is big?
   It might be correct to check and hope that the bet comes on your left, then you can check-raise and build a big pot.

9. Is this play recommended in tough games?

No.

10. Why?

You are now more likely to be up against a bigger flush draw and the original bettor is more likely to reraise.

# Raising

1. Give five reasons to raise.
    A.  To get more money in the pot.
    B.  To drive players out.
    C.  To bluff (or semi-bluff).
    D.  To get a free card.
    E.  To gain information.

2. If you think you have the bettor beat is it generally correct to raise even if you risk driving out players behind you?
    Yes.

3. A raise on the flop to drive players out will work only under what condition?
    This will work only against those players who have not yet had a chance to call the original bet.

4. Why is a raise often correct even if you are not sure that you have the best hand?
    If you do hold the best hand, or if your hand becomes the best hand, your raise may have stopped other opponents from drawing out on you.

5. Example?
    Suppose you raised before the flop with A♦4♦, the flop is T♦4♣2♠. If someone on your right bets, a raise is often correct, especially if you think that the raise will buy you a free card.

6. When can you occasionally raise as a pure bluff?
    When you are playing in very tough games.

7.Why?

Because players are capable of folding in big pots without calling one last bet.

8. Are these plays recommended?

No, not usually.

9. Why?

They succeed rarely and are expensive when they fail.

10. When is the one time that a bluff-raise can be used in a weaker game?

When you think that your opponent is bluffing, but also think that your hand is even worse.

11. Example?

Your flush draw did not get there, but the hand was played in such a fashion that you are fairly sure your opponent was also on a flush draw.

12. Give an example of raising as a semi-bluff.

You have A♣4♣, the flop is J♦3♣8♠, and everyone checks. If the next card is the 5♣, you should usually raise if someone bets.

13. Another example?

You can raise as a semi-bluff almost any time that you pick up a back-door flush draw after calling on the flop with top pair. (But again, make this play only against someone who is capable of folding.)

14. How likely is it that someone will fold for a raise?
    The answer is based on the answers to the following three questions:
    A.   How capable is this person of folding a big hand?
    B.   How likely is he to be semi-bluffing?
    C.   How are you perceived by this individual?

15. When is raising to get a free card best done?
    When you are in late position and the bet is smaller than the bets on succeeding rounds.

16. When should raising to gain information be done?
    Only rarely, usually just in heads-up situations.

17. Is this raise worth it?
    Probably not, as you usually have to "pay" too much for the information.

# Heads-Up on Fifth Street

1. When is it correct to bluff?
   When your hand can't win by checking, and the odds you are getting from the pot compared to the chance your opponent will call are favorable.

2. Give an example if you have been calling all the way?
   A significant card that appears to help you but does not, such as a flush card on fifth street, may make a bluff correct.

3. Give an example if you have been betting all the way?
   You might try a bluff on the end regardless of the last card.

4. What else must you consider?
   Whether your opponent is capable of folding a decent hand.

5. When is it correct to bet a legitimate hand on the end in last position?
   When you think you will have the best hand at least 55 percent of the time *that you are called.*

6. If your opponent has come out betting, when should you call?
   You should call only if your chances compare favorably with the pot odds.

7. To raise, how much of a favorite must you be?
   Usually about 2-to-1. (Except for bluff-raises.)

8. What is another way to decide that a raise is generally correct?
   When you think you will have the best hand 55 percent of the time that your raise is called.

9. What is an exception to this rule?

If you think your opponent has the same hand as you and you believe that your raise will sometimes make him fold.

10. What options do you have in heads-up, last round situations?
    A.  To bet.
    B.  To check with the intention of folding.
    C.  To check with the intention of calling.
    D.  To check with the intention of raising.

11. When you have a good hand, whether to check-raise or come right out betting depends on what three probabilities?
    A.  The chance that you will be called if you bet, assuming that you won't be raised.
    B.  The chance that your opponent will bet if you check, but will not call your raise.
    C.  The chance that he will bet and then call your raise.

12. When does going for a check-raise become the correct strategy?

When the second probability added to twice the third probability exceeds the first probability.

13. What are some hints that should help you determine whether a check-raise is correct?
    A.  Is the river card likely to give someone a second-best hand that he might think is the best hand?
    B.  Is your opponent the type of player who would always try to pick up the pot if you check, but is not likely to call with a weak hand?
    C.  Consider whether your opponent is afraid of being check-raised.
    D.  Consider your previous play.

14. When is it the best strategy to check and call?

When your opponent will bet with any of the hands that he will call with, plus some hands that are worse (usually bluffs).

15. What else does a check do for you in this spot?
    It eliminates the possibility of a raise.

16. Against an opponent who will call your bet more often than he will bet himself, what should you do?
    You should bet.

17. What if you are an underdog when he calls?
    This bet is still correct as long as you were going to call his bet anyway, or when folding would be a close decision if you check and he bets.

18. Example?
    You have T♣9♦, and when all the cards are out, the board is T♥T♠Q♠4♠5♦. By betting, you will cause some timid players to call with a queen or an overpair, which they probably would not have bet.

19. When should you check and fold?
    When you are a definite underdog, think a bluff would be unprofitable, and do not think the probability that your opponent is bluffing warrants a call.

20. Example?
    You have middle pair and have not improved. Against an opponent who hardly ever bluffs and normally would not bet anything less than top pair, you should fold.

# Miscellaneous Topics

1. Give three examples of when someone absolutely has you beat on the river?
   A. Suppose the flop is Q♥6♠2♥ and you have A♣A♠. There is a bet, you raise, and someone cold calls behind you. The turn card is a blank. Again there is a bet, you raise, and the same player cold calls. If the flush card comes on the end, it is now almost impossible for you to have the best hand.
   B. You are in a multiway pot, and there are no drawing opportunities other than two flush cards. If a flush card appears, you are most likely beaten.
   C. Someone raises on the flop, especially against two or three people, then checks on fourth street after everyone else checks (when a non-flush card hits), but bets on the river if the flush card comes.

2. If you semi-bluff on the flop and are called, should you continue betting on fourth street?
   This depends on the situation. If you bet on the flop, a lot of players will call and then routinely throw their hands away for the next bet. However, if you always bet again, many of your opponents will pick up this pattern and will call or even raise you on fourth street.

3. What does this mean?
   You should give up on many of your semi-bluffs once the turn comes.

4. Suppose you flop an open-end straight draw and two flush cards are also on board. Is it correct to bet?
   If you are against a small number of opponents a bet is usually the correct strategy.

5. What about a hand that gives you an inside straight draw with two overcards on the flop?

> You should play this hand strongly, especially against a small number of opponents, and be inclined to bet it a second time regardless of the fourth street card.

6. Betting in late position on the flop, are you likely to get a free card?

> Yes, most of the time. If you bet on the flop and are called, most players will tend to check to you on fourth street.

7. In this situation, should you be concerned about a check-raise?

> Yes.

8. What is this a function of?

> More so the opponents that you are up against, rather than of the cards that appeared on the flop.

9. Is it correct to play flush draws when a pair is on board?

> Since you may run into a full house, the main thing to consider is how much money is in the pot. In other words, the pot should be offering you somewhat better odds than if there were no pair showing.

10. What else is important to consider?

> Which pair and off-card are on the flop.

11. Example?

> If the flop is J♣J♠T♣, someone already may have flopped a full house. On the other hand, if the flop is 9♥9♠2♥, it is unlikely that you are looking at a full house.

12. Should you call with a straight draw if two flush cards have flopped?

> Many of the same ideas apply. Basically, since you may run into a flush, you need better than normal pot odds to call.

13. If the board pairs on fourth street, should drawing hands be thrown away?

Rarely. However, you need somewhat better odds than normal to continue playing. In addition, consider which card has paired and what the other two cards are.

14. Suppose the board pairs on fourth street, someone bets, you are next, and there are several players behind you, what must you be aware of?

You may be raised if you call. Thus you may be forced to put a lot of money in the pot on a 4-to-1 shot.

15. If there has been no raise before the flop, how should you play from the flop on?

Tighter, since more possible hands may be out and you are getting smaller pot odds.

16. Example?

Suppose the flop comes with a small pair. If there was an early-position raiser and a couple of callers, you could be fairly sure that no one has a third card of the appropriate rank. However, this would not necessarily be the case if there was no raise, especially if many players took the flop (or if the raise came after many players had already called).

17. What if a two flush flops?

A. Play your good hands more aggressively since there is a better chance that you will be called.
B. Virtually never slowplay.
C. If your hand is mediocre but normally worth a bet, it is usually correct to check. You might run into fancy raises or be outdrawn even if you currently have the best hand.

18. Is it profitable to bluff when a pair flops?

Yes, especially if the flop does not include a straight or flush draw.

19. What should you do if a good player "plays back" at you?

You should consider taking it to a third bet and then betting the rest of the hand. However, don't do this automatically.

20. How else can you bluff at flops that contain a pair?

You can make a "delayed bluff." Instead of betting immediately when a pair flops, it is often best to check. If a good player bets from a late position and you think he is capable of bluffing in this spot, you can call if no one else has entered the pot. Assuming that no one calls behind you, you can bet into your opponent on fourth street.

21. Example?

In a many-handed pot, the flop comes Q♠6♦6♥. You check from early position, a strong player bets in a late position, you call, and there are no other players. It is now correct to go ahead and bet on the turn, no matter what card hits.

22. What should you keep in mind when you play a pair in the hole?

If you do not make trips when an overcard flops — particularly if the overcard is an ace — you are in trouble.

23. When is this especially true?

In a multiway pot.

24. Example?

You have Q♣Q♦ against four opponents. A king flops, and someone bets into you. If you showed strength before the flop, you are almost always beaten.

25. What is an exception to this fold?

If the bettor is the type of player who will almost always go for a check-raise if he flops a hand as strong as top pair.

26. In a heads-up situation, do you automatically discard your hand when an overcard flops?

No.

27. Example?

You have J♣J♠, the flop comes K♦T♠4♣ and your opponent bets. If he is equally likely to bet a ten as a king, you should continue to play.

28. Can you semi-bluff with a pair in the hole?

Yes. You may bet into overcards in the hope of folding out medium pairs. Notice that this is not exactly a semi-bluff.

29. Example?

Suppose the flop is A♣K♠2♦ and you hold 8♣8♦. Your bet might cause an opponent with 99, TT, JJ, or QQ to fold, especially if he plays "weak tight."

30. Suppose you have 9♣6♦ in the blind and get a free play against three or four opponents. The flop comes Q♦9♥2♠. Is it correct to bet in order to stop free cards form beating you? Or is this a check-and-fold situation?

It is a close decision between betting, checking and calling, and checking and folding.

31. What if your kicker is good — that is, it is above a queen?

A bet would be correct.

32. Suppose the flop is the same, but you hold T♦T♠. How should this hand be played?

Since you can now beat all middle pairs, you should bet on the flop and, if you are not raised, bet again on fourth street.

33. What if the flop includes two suited cards?

If the pot is short-handed, usually bet. If several players are in, bet only if one of your tens is of the appropriate suit.

34. What if you are against several players who will play any ace? Check and fold any pair below aces if an ace flops, unless the pot odds justify chasing.

35. How do you play against a loose, wild, and extremely aggressive player?
    If he acts after you do, you must be very selective of the hands you play. If you act after him and you are going to play, be prepared to reraise to punish him for his extra aggressive tendencies.

36. Where do you usually want to sit if there is a maniac in the game?
    On his left unless there are some wise players in the game who will not tolerate your strategy.

37. What is the advantage of being on his right?
    It gives you the opportunity to limp in before the flop or to check to him on the later streets.

38. What is the only reason to be on his left?
    To isolate him.

39. What hands do you play against a maniac who is raising almost every hand?
    Play those hands that can win showdowns without improving. This includes hands like A9 and KT.

40. Suppose you have Q♥Q♠. You open for two bets, and someone else makes it three bets. What should you do if an ace or a king appears on the flop?
    You generally should check and fold.

41. What if the flop looks favorable?
    Be prepared to check and call all the way.

42. What is an exception to only calling before the flop, as opposed to reraising?

 It is when you believe that your opponent may believe that you might be stealing.

43. When does this usually occur?

 You are first in from a late position, or just by circumstance you have been raising a lot.

44. Suppose the flop looks favorable, but you hold 9♠9♣?

 You still should play as before.

45. How should you play top pair if a three-flush flops and you are against a few opponents?

 You generally should bet as you cannot afford to give a free card.

46. What if you are against a lot of players and you are early to act?

 It is probably best to check and call.

47. What if several players have already passed?

 You should usually bet.

48. If a three-flush flops and you have a "high suited card," how high does this card need to be for you to keep playing?

 High suited card means one of the top two of that particular suit.

49. Against a few opponents, what does a suited flop sometimes allow you to do?

 Bluff.

50. What should happen?

 As long as your opponents are reasonable players, they won't call your bet on the flop unless they have at least top pair or one of the two suited cards.

51. Should you bluff into several opponents when you see a flop with a medium two card comibnation, such as J♣T♦3♠?

No. There are just too many ways that a JT or a T9 can hit your opponents.

52. What type of hand should you bet on fourth street?

Hands that, if already beaten, have no outs.

53. What if your hand has outs?

Tend to check.

54. Example?

You hold A♣A♠, a third suited card comes on fourth street, and neither of your aces is of that suit. Against a typical opponent, the correct play is to bet and then fold if you are raised.

55. But what if you make two pair when the third suited card hits on fourth street?

The best play is usually to check and call.

56. Example?

You start with K♦3♦, and on fourth street the board is K♣J♥7♣3♣. If you are first to act, you generally should check and call.

57. What if you are against someone who plays as instructed in this text?

It may be wrong to bet and fold when it appears you have no outs.

58. What is the correct play if you have two pair or a set on the turn, a third suited card hits, and your opponent bets into you?

The correct play usually is to raise.

59. What is the second important concept concerning fourth-street play?

>You should be betting good hands on the flop, but then frequently check-raising with them on the turn.

60. Why should this be routine strategy?

>You will be giving up on many hands on fourth street. That is, you won't follow through on most of your semi-bluffs and/or the other weak hands that you routinely bet on the flop. Therefore, to avoid giving your hand away, you also must check a lot of good hands.

61. What does this mean?

>When first to act you probably should check on fourth street as much as 60 percent of the time with your good and bad hands alike, as long as free cards are not a major problem and your opponents are aggressive.

62. What if the game is very loose?

>In this situation you won't be making many semi-bluff type bets on the flop, so it won't be necessary to balance your strategy.

63. Should you be afraid of cinch hands in most situations?

>No.

64. Suppose you have Q♦J♠ and flop two pair with a small card. You bet and get two callers, one before you and one after you. A nine — which could give someone a straight — comes on fourth street, and the first person bets into you. How should you play?

>You should not fold. This person could easily be betting a hand like jacks and nines, or a pair and a straight draw. Your best play is usually to raise.

65. What is a play that expert players make against mediocre opposition on fourth street?

They will bluff from an early position into several opponents, all of whom have checked on the flop.

66. When does this play work best?

When the turn card is not an overcard or a third suited card.

67. What is another idea to keep in mind?

Some of your opponents are more likely to be weak if they bet the flop, as opposed to check-raising.

68. On the flop, suppose there is some chance that you have the best hand and that everyone will fold if you bet, but if you don't have the best hand, you have little chance of improvement. What should you do?

Frequently bet.

69. Example?

You call a raise from the big blind with a pair of sixes, are against two opponents, and the flop comes A♦T♣5♠. You should strongly consider betting. If raised, almost always fold, and if called, usually check on the next round.

70. You are against a small number of players, flop a good but not great hand, and someone to your surprise bets into you. What should you do?

Frequently just call on the flop and fourth street, and then raise on the river.

# Playing in Loose Games

1. Against bad players is it detrimental to mull over your decisions?
   Yes, it probably is.

2. Why?
   When you sit there and think you encourage bad players to play better against you.

3. What is it that you don't want to portray?
   That you are capable of throwing away good hands for one more bet and that you look at every single decision critically.

4. When do you extract the most money from your opponents?
   When you put them in a position to make big mistakes.

5. What should you do in a loose passive game where many players see the flop and then play poorly after that?
   A.  Play more hands, especially for a single bet.
   B.  Frequently keep it to a single bet before the flop.

6. With a hand that is pretty good but not great, what happens if you don't raise and cost yourself a *little* bit of money at that point?
   You gain it back *plus* some because had you made the pot bigger there would be less opportunities for your opponents to make significant mistakes later on.

7. What if you're playing against extremely terrible opponents?
   It's hard not to raise with pretty good hands even though you're costing yourself money on the later streets.

8. What is a reason not to play K♦5♦?
   It can be a problem if a king flops.

9. What if you are a good player?

You won't get trapped. You should be able to play K♦5♦, flop a king, and still often fold.

10. In a multiway pot when is it often correct strategy to call with bottom pair?

If there was a raise, but not if there was not a raise.

11. If the game is good, what should you do?

Play more hands, specifically suited hands, but only if it appears that you can get in cheaply with them.

12. If you are in a loose passive game, where they usually call, but only occasionally raise, what hands can you play under the gun?

Axs, J9s, anything better, and all pairs.

13. What about AK or AQ?

You often shouldn't raise in spots where you would raise in tougher, tighter games.

14. In a big pot why can it be right to bet a hand that you know is beat?

Because it's important to increase your chance to win the pot.

15. Suppose you have A♦K♦, you are on the button, and there are seven people in for a triple bet. The flop comes A♣9♦4♠, and the player on your right is the first to bet. What should you do?

You should often just call and go for the raise on fourth street.

16. Is it important that your hand be suited?

Yes, it is a giant advantage.

17. What is a reason to raise with flush cards?

If you flop the draw, by your making the pot bigger people will now play hands that can't win against your hand if you hit it.

18. What if the other players are terrible?

There is no reason to make this raise in order to attract their call on the flop because they will stay in anyway.

19. For a raise with AQ in early position to be correct what do you need to accomplish?

You must be able to limit the pot to only a small number of players.

20. If a tough player on your right bets, there is a bad player to your left, and the situation is close between raising and calling, what should you do?

You should not raise.

# Playing Short-Handed

1. What must you realize?
   An individual could have the best of it by always betting.

2. When you are in the big blind and playing heads-up, what are the two things that you should do?
   A.   Call quite a bit more than one out of three times.
   B.   Reraise frequently.

3. In a heads-up match in the big blind what hands should you play against an aggressive opponent?
   Any pair, any ace, any two cards that are both nine or higher, any other straight flush combination with no gaps or just one gap (except for 42s and 32s), any king little suited that is not already covered, and perhaps a few others such as J8s, 98, or 97.

4. When do you call on the flop?
   Anytime you have something reasonable, as well as with some other hands that don't appear reasonable.

5. Why do you reraise out of the blind when playing short-handed?
   You do it for future hands, not necessarily for that current hand.

6. What does this mean if you are against an aggressive player who is going to constantly take advantage of his position?
   You must reraise him more than might seem logical.

7. So how often should you reraise in a short-handed game when you are defending out of the big blind?
   You should probably reraise about one out of four times that you play.

8. Assuming you reraised, what should you be prepared to do on the flop?

A lot of betting.

9. Example?

If you reraise with J♥T♥ and the flop is 9♥4♠2♦, you go ahead and bet.

10. What happens when it is three-handed and the player on the button raises?

The combined calling frequency of the blinds should be only a little more than it was for the big blind (when playing heads-up) and the little blind should play about half as often as the big blind.

11. On the flop against a very aggressive player who is automatically going to try to steal, what should you do?

Pretend that the top card isn't there or turn it into a deuce in your mind.

12. Example?

You have Q♠T♥ and the flop is A♣9♦4♠. Just change it to 9♦4♠2♣ and continue to play since you have two "overcards" and a backdoor straight draw.

13. Should you be betting every time?

No, you don't want to make your strategy completely obvious.

14. What is another idea that is important in short-handed play?

To throw in a raise with a hand that seems like it is only worth a call.

15. Why do you do this?

To thwart the strategy of players who are doing a lot of semi-bluffing.

16. Example?
    You have Q♠T♥ and the flop is Q♥8♦5♣. The right play might be to call your opponent's bet on the flop and then to raise him on fourth street even though your hand only looks like a "pay off" hand.

17. What if you are against someone who will always bluff on the river if you only call on the turn?
    Then it doesn't do you any good to raise.

18. What if he is a real aggressive player and will reraise with many hands?
    Then you are better off just calling.

19. When should you just call with some hands if you are first in on the button?
    When the players in the blinds are very loose or at least highly apt to defend their blinds.

20. What are three ideal hands to do this with?
    Small pairs, small suited connectors, or a hand like A♣6♥.

21. What is another reason to just call before the flop?
    You make it more likely that you will steal the pot if they both check on the flop.

22. What if you are one off the button?
    You should not usually make this play. Now you fold the A♣6♥.

23. Why should you frequently lead on the flop?
    It is highly beneficial to be able to bet out and sometimes pick up the pot.

24. How do you preserve this highly profitable play?
    By not automatically checking to the raiser when you have something.

25. Heads-up, what hands does this include?
    A pair (including bottom pair) or a draw.

26. Are we saying that you should never check-raise?
    No. If your strategy was to never check-raise, your opponent would begin to realize that when you do check you don't have anything.

27. Do you call as much on fourth street as you do on the flop?
    No, except against the wildest players.

28. Does this mean you revert to a tight strategy?
    No, you still have to do a fair amount of calling.

29. If you are last to act (on the flop) and are against an extremely aggressive player, what should you do?
    Slowplay some hands that don't seem to merit this strategy.

30. When making this play what do you need to keep in mind?
    The lower the hand, the less likely this tricky play is worth it.

31. On fifth street, since it often doesn't take that much to win, what must you do?
    Pay off with a lot of hands.

32. What if you are first to act (on fifth street) and you have a mediocre hand?
    It is usually better to try to induce a bluff.

33. What happens if your opponents only see you thinking in borderline situations?
    They will have a big advantage.

# Reading Hands

1. What is the most common way to read hands?

Analyze the meaning of an opponent's check, bet or raise, and look at the exposed cards to try to judge from them what his entire hand might be. You then combine the plays he has made *throughout the hand* with the exposed cards and come to a determination about his most likely hand.

2. Is it a mistake to put an opponent on a specific hand early and to stick to your initial conclusion no matter how things develop?

Yes.

3. Suppose when two suited cards appear on the flop an opponent raises after there has been a bet and a couple of callers, but then checks on the turn when a blank hits. What is a likely hand for him?

A flush draw.

4. In practice, what do most players try to determine?

Whether an opponent has a bad hand, a mediocre hand, a good hand, or a great hand.

5. If your opponent bets on the end, what type of hand is he unlikely to have?

A mediocre hand.

6. What is a complimentary way to read hands?

To work backward.

7. If the last card is a deuce and an opponent who has just been calling suddenly bets, is it likely that he has a set of deuces?

No. It does not seem possible that he would have called this far with only two deuces in the hole.

8. Suppose the flop comes K♠Q♦2♣. The first player bets, and the second player raises. A third person, who is also in an early position and is a solid but not overly aggressive player raises again. Also suppose that several opponents remain to act behind the reraiser, and that this reraiser had just called before the flop. Is the reraiser trying for a free card?

No.

9. Could the reraiser have a set?

No. He would have raised before the flop with KK or QQ, but would not play 22 from so early a position.

10. Does the reraiser have AKs, AK, or KQs?

No. He probably would have raised before the flop with these hands.

11. Would he make it three bets with KJ♠, KJ, KT♠, or KT?

No.

12. What possibility is left?

KQ.

13. When you can't put a person on a hand, but have reduced his possible holdings to a limited number, what do you do to determine the chance of his having certain hands rather than others?

Mathematics.

14. Suppose an early position player calls and then reraises. You read him as the type of player who will initially call and then reraise only with AA, KK, AKs, or AK. What are the chances that your opponent does not hold a pair?

He will get AA or KK 0.9 percent of the time and AKs or AK 1.2 percent of the time. By comparing these two probabilities you deduce that the chances are 4-to-3 that your opponent does not hold a pair.

15. Suppose you have J♠J♣, the flop comes A♥T♠3♣, and your opponent bets. What should you do if you think your opponent is equally likely to have a ten as an ace?

> You should at least call.

16. If the turn card is another ace and your opponent bets again, what is your play?

> To raise if you know that this opponent would still bet if he had only a ten.

17. What is another factor in reading hands and deciding how to play your own hand?

> The number of players in the pot.

18. In addition to the bettor, if there is also a caller ahead of you, what must you do?

> Tighten up significantly because you no longer have the extra equity that the bettor may be bluffing.

# Psychology

1. What do we mean by the "psychology of poker?"
   Getting into your opponents' heads, analyzing how they think, figuring out what they think you think, and even determining what they think you think they think.

2. Suppose you bluff at a flop that contains a pair and are raised by a strong opponent who knows you would bluff at this flop. What may be the correct play for you?
   To reraise and then bet again on the turn if necessary.

3. Would you make this play against a weak player?
   No.

4. When an opponent bets on the end in a situation where he is sure that you are going to call, is he bluffing?
   No.

5. Example?
   You bet when all the cards are out and a player raises you.

6. Is folding in similar situations correct on fourth street?
   No. Tough players will raise on the turn if they hold a mediocre hand that has some potential to become a very strong hand.

7. When might your opponent be bluffing?
   If he bets when there appears to be a good *chance* that you will fold.

8. Example?

No one bets on the flop and a small card hits on the turn. If one of your opponents now bets, and he is the type of player who would try to pick up the pot with nothing, it may be correct to call (or raise) with a relatively weak hand.

9. In deciding whether to bet, what else is important to consider?

What your opponent thinks *you* have.

10. If your opponent suspects a strong hand, what should you do?

Bluff more.

11. Example?

You raise before the flop with A♦Q♦, three rags flop, and the last card is a king. If you have been betting all the way, it would be difficult for anyone to call on the end with only a small pair.

12. What if your opponent suspects that you are weak?

You should not try to bluff, as you will get caught. But you should bet your fair hands for value.

13. Should you ever intentionally make an incorrect play?

Yes.

14. Why?

You are trying to affect the thinking of your opponents for future hands.

15. Example?

You occasionally can make it three bets before the flop with a hand like 7♥6♥. Assuming that your opponents see your hand in a showdown, they should be less inclined to steal against you in a similar situation when rags flop.

16. Give another example of this type of play.
    You can throw in an extra raise early in a hand with cards that don't really warrant it.

17. What are you trying to do?
    Give the *illusion of action.*

18. Example?
    You can occasionally raise the pot with a hand like 5♦3♦.

19. When should you not make this play?
    In loose games where you are against people who play too many hands and go too far with their hands.

20. With what type of players do these types of plays work well against?
    Players who are good enough to try to take advantage of their new found knowledge, but who are not good enough to realize that you know this.

# Questions and Answers

# Afterthought

Again, these questions are not designed as a replacement for the material in the text. Their purpose is to help keep you sharp between complete readings of *Hold 'em Poker for Advanced Players*. We recommend that when you believe you have become a winning hold 'em player that you reread the text material every other month and review the questions about once a week. Also, remember to cover the answers and to think through those questions that you have trouble with. In addition, attempt to relate the questions to recent hands that you have played, and try to determine which concepts were the correct ones to apply.

Another thing to keep in mind, as has been mentioned several times in this book, is that Texas hold 'em is an extremely complicated form of poker. This means that you should be a student of hold 'em for life. Some forms of poker are much more simple, and you can master them in a relatively short period of time. One reason for this is that only a small number of situations can develop, and in time, you will know exactly what the correct strategy is for virtually every hand that you play. Unfortunately, hold 'em is not this way. It takes a long time to become an expert hold 'em player. That is why continuous review of these questions (and the rest of the material in this book) is an absolute necessity.

# Conclusion

One difference between Texas hold 'em and other forms of poker is that most of the money is not won or lost on the first round of play. It is true that your decisions concerning which two cards to play and exactly how to play them are very important. However, this is not enough to make you into a winning player. That is why play on the flop and after the flop received so much emphasis. On the other hand, those of you who make many significant misplays on your first two cards will be losers.

Perhaps the least known advice given in this text concerns play out of the blinds and some of the fourth-street strategies. In fact, we suspect that some readers will think that we are too aggressive in the little blind and that we do not bet enough on fourth street. Rest assured that this is not the case. Both of us know not only from a theoretical point of view, but also from much practical experience, that these approaches are absolutely correct in today's modern game against typical hold 'em opponents.

In the introduction to *Hold 'em Poker for Advanced Players,* we mentioned that hold 'em literature seems to be flooding the market. Unfortunately, most of this material is either not accurate or extremely lacking in many aspects of the game. This is why we expanded the sections explaining how to play in loose games and how to play short-handed. Virtually all of the material that we had seen in these areas was incomplete at best and/or misguided at worst. It seemed as if many of the concepts which drive proper strategy in these situations were either being reversed or not addressed. All of this is now corrected.

We believe this book will have a major impact on those of you who read and study it, as well as on the games themselves. As we stated before, there will be more tough players around, meaning that some games will be harder to beat. We also expect this text to continue to be a significant contributor to the future growth of hold 'em, making more games available so the expert player will have more games from which to choose. Consequently, the book should benefit those of you who make a commitment to studying the ideas that it contains.

# Appendix A: Probability

With experience, most players know the approximate odds of making various hands. Only in close situations is it important to be accurate. Even here, a mistake is not tragic. However, we will note some of the more important and interesting probabilities.

A classic mistake that many players make is miscalculating their chance when there are two cards to come. For instance, if a player can catch nine cards to make his hand, he knows he is a 38-to-9 underdog on the next round, assuming 47 unseen cards. However, he incorrectly doubles his outs to 18 when figuring his odds for both rounds and thus arrives at 29-to-18 (38.3 percent), a figure 3.3 percent too high. We will not bother you with the proper technique for calculating these odds. Instead, we have provided a chart that shows the exact probability of making your hand with two cards to come, assuming 47 unseen cards.

## Probability of Completing Hand

| No. of Outs | Percentage | No. of Outs | Percentage |
|:-----------:|:----------:|:-----------:|:----------:|
| 20 | 67.5 | 10 | 38.4 |
| 19 | 65.0 | 9 | 35.0[2] |
| 18 | 62.4 | 8 | 31.5[3] |
| 17 | 59.8 | 7 | 27.8 |
| 16 | 57.0 | 6 | 24.1 |
| 15 | 54.1[1] | 5 | 20.3 |
| 14 | 51.2 | 4 | 16.5[4] |
| 13 | 48.1 | 3 | 12.5 |
| 12 | 45.0 | 2 | 8.4 |
| 11 | 41.7 | 1 | 4.4 |

[1] Straight flush draw     [2] Flush draw
[3] Straight draw     [4] Two pair or gut-shot draw

To change a percentage to odds (to 1), subtract the specified percentage in the table from 100 and divide the result by this same percentage. For example, to change 27.8 percent to odds, subtract 27.8 from 100 giving 72.2. Then divide the result by 27.8 giving 2.597 (to 1).

$$72.2 = 100 - 27.8$$

Thus 27.8 percent is the same as 2.597-to-1.

$$2.597 = \frac{72.2}{27.8}$$

If you hold a wired pair, you will flop three-of-a-kind or better 11.8 percent of the time. If you hold AK, you will flop at least one ace or one king 32.4 percent of the time. If you hold two unmatched cards, you will flop a split two pair 2.02 percent of the time.

If you hold two suited cards, you will flop a flush 0.8 percent of the time, and a four-flush 10.9 percent of the time. Two suited cards will make a flush about 6.5 percent of the time, but this figure assumes that you will stay in with a three-flush on the flop, hoping to catch two running cards.

In a 10-handed game, the chance that someone holds an ace and another card of a specified suit is about 9 percent; however, this figure decreases if you flop a four-flush. Thus your king-high flush will be beaten by an ace-high flush less than 6 percent of the time (when there is a three-flush on board).

You are two and one-third times as likely to be dealt an AK (or any two unmatched cards) as a pair. Consequently, a player who will raise with AA, KK, or AK is more likely to have specifically AK than the other two hands combined.

If you flop trips, you will wind up with a full house or better 33 percent of the time. If you flop two pair, a four-straight, a four-flush, and so on use the chart to determine the probability of making your hand.

# Appendix B: Glossary

**Action:** The betting in a particular hand or game. A game with a lot of action is a game with a lot of betting. The player who starts the action is the player who makes the first bet.

**Active player:** A player still in the pot.

**All-in:** Having all one's money in the pot.

**Back door:** Three cards to a flush or a straight after five cards have been dealt. In general, the term is used for a hand made on the end which a player was not originally trying to make.

**Bad beat:** Having a hand that is a big favorite defeated as the result of a lucky draw, especially when the person drawing was playing incorrectly by being in the pot in the first place.

**Bad game:** A game in which your opponents are too good for you to expect to win; a game in which you're an underdog.

**Bankroll:** The amount of money you have available to wager.

**Belly buster:** A draw to an inside-straight. Also called a gut shot.

**Best of it:** A situation in which a wager can be expected to be profitable in the long run.

**Bet:** To put money in the pot before anyone else on any given round.

**Bettor:** The person who first puts money in the pot on any given round.

**Bet for value:** To bet in order to be called by a lesser hand. You are betting to make money, not to make your opponents fold.

**Big slick:** Ace-king.

**Blank:** A card that is not of any value to a player's hand.

**Blind:** A forced bet that one or more players must make to start the action on the first round of betting. The blind rotates around the table with each new deal. The person whose turn it is to bet is said to be in the blind.

**Bluff:** A bet or raise with a hand you do not think is the best hand.

**Board:** The community cards in the center of the table.

**Bottom pair:** Pairing the lowest card on board.

**Busted hand:** A hand that does not develop into anything of value.

**Button:** When there is a house dealer, as in the card rooms of Las Vegas, the *button* is a round disc that rotates around the table to represent the dealer for the purposes of indicating which player is to be first to act.

**Buy in:** The minimum amount of money required to sit down in a particular game.

**Card room:** The area in a casino where poker (and sometimes panguingue) is played.

**Call:** To put in the pot an amount of money equal to an opponent's bet or raise.

**Call a raise cold:** To call a double bet — that is, a bet and a raise.

**Caller:** A person who calls a bet or raise.

**Chase:** To continue in a hand trying to outdraw an opponent's hand you are quite sure is better than yours.

**Check:** To decline to bet when it is your turn.

**Check-raise:** To check and then raise after an opponent bets.

**Chip:** A round token in various denominations representing money. Among many professional gamblers it is also called a check.

**Cinch:** The best possible hand, given the cards on board, when all the cards are out.

**Come hand:** A hand that has not yet been made, with more cards still to be dealt. Thus, a four-card flush would be a come hand.

**Community cards:** The cards dealt face up in the center of the table that are shared by all active players.

**Crying call:** A call with a hand you think has a small chance of winning.

**Cut the pot:** To take a percentage from each pot as the profits for the person or the casino running the game.

**Dead hand:** A hand a player may not continue to play because of an irregularity.

**Dead money:** Money put in the pot by players who have already folded their hands.

**Drawing dead:** Drawing to try to make a hand that cannot possibly win because an opponent already holds a bigger hand. A player drawing to make a flush when an opponent already has a full house is drawing dead.

**Draw out:** To improve your hand so that it beats an opponent who had a better hand than yours prior to your draw.

**Double belly buster:** *See* Open-ended straight.

**Early position:** A position on a round of betting in which you must act before most of the other players.

**Edge:** An advantage over an opponent.

**Effective odds:** The ratio of the total amount of money you expect to win if you make your hand to the total amount of bets you will have to call to continue from the present round of betting to the end of the hand.

**Equity:** The value of a particular hand or combination of cards.

**Expectation:** The average profit (or loss) of any bet over the long run.

**Favorite:** In poker, before all the cards are out, a hand that has the best chance of winning.

**Family pot:** A pot in which most of the players at the table are involved.

**Fifth street:** The fifth and final community card on board.

**Fill:** To draw a card that makes a hand. For example, to fill a flush is to draw a fifth card of that suit.

**Fill up:** To make a full house.

**Flat call:** To call a bet without raising.

**Flop:** The first three exposed community cards, which are dealt simultaneously. The word is also used as a verb. For example, to flop a set is to make three-of-a-kind on the flop.

**Flush:** Five cards of the same suit.

**Fold:** To drop out of a pot rather than call a bet or raise.

**Four-flush:** Four cards to a flush.

**Four-of-a-kind:** Four cards of the same rank. Four jacks is four-of-a-kind.

**Fourth street:** The fourth community card on board.

**Free card:** A card that a player gets without having to call a bet.

**Free roll:** A situation where two players have the same hand but one of them has a chance to make a better hand.

**Full house:** Three cards of one rank and two of another. A♣A♥A♦9♠9♥ is a full house.

**Giving a hand away:** Playing your hand in such a way that your opponents should know what you have.

**Good game:** A game in which there are enough players worse than you for you to be a substantial favorite.

**Gut shot:** A draw to an inside straight. Also called a belly buster.

**Heads-up:** Playing against a single opponent.

**Hourly rate:** The amount of money a player expects to win per hour on average.

**Implied odds:** The ratio of the total amount of money you expect to win if you make your hand to the bet you must now call to continue in the hand.

**Inside straight:** A straight which can be made only with a card of one rank, usually somewhere in the middle of the straight. When you hold ten-nine-seven-six, only an eight will give you a straight. Thus, you are drawing to an inside straight, or you have an inside-straight draw.

**Kicker:** A side card.

**Late position:** A position on a round of betting in which you act after most of the other players have acted.

**Legitimate hand:** A hand with value; a hand that is not a bluffing hand.

**Limit:** The amount a player may bet or raise on any round of betting.

**Limp in:** To call a bet rather than raise. (This usually applies only to the first round of betting.)

**Live one:** A loose, weak player with a lot of money to lose.

**Lock:** A cinch hand. A hand that cannot lose.

**Long shot:** A hand that has little chance of being made.

**Loose:** Playing more hands than the norm.

**Loose game:** A game with a lot of players in most pots.

**Mathematical expectation:** The mathematical calculation of what a bet can be expected to win or lose on average.

**Middle pair:** Pairing the second highest card on board.

**Middle position:** A position on a round of betting somewhere in the middle. In a ten-handed game middle position generally refers to those players four or five seats to the left of the big blind.

**Muck:** To discard a hand; the pile of discards in front of the dealer.

**Multiway pot:** A pot in which more than two players are involved.

**Negative expectation:** The amount a wager may be expected to lose on average. A play with negative expectation is a play that will lose money over the long run.

**Nuts:** The best possible hand at any given point in a pot.

**Odds:** The chance, expressed mathematically, that an event will occur. Also, in the term *pot odds,* the ratio of the size of the pot to the amount of the bet you must call to continue.

**Off-suit:** Not of the same suit.

**On the come:** Playing a hand that has not yet been made. For instance, if you bet with four cards to a flush, you are betting on the come.

**On tilt:** Playing much worse than usual because, for one reason or another, you have become emotionally upset.

**Open-ended straight:** Four cards to a straight, which can be made with cards of two different ranks. Thus, nine-eight-seven-six is an open-ended straight, which can be made with either a ten or a five. Theoretically, jack-nine-eight-seven-five is also open-ended in that either a ten or a six will make the hand. The latter hand is also called a double belly buster.

**Outs:** Cards which will improve your hand. Also, ways of improving your hand. The term is used particularly in reference to a hand that needs to improve to become the best hand.

**Overcall:** A call of a bet after another player has already called.

**Overcard:** A card higher than any card on the flop, or any card higher than those in your hand.

**Overpair:** A wired pair that is higher than any card on board.

**Pair:** Two cards of the same rank. Two eights is a *pair.*

**Pass:** To check. Also, to fold.

**Pay off:** To call a bet or raise when you don't think you have the best hand.

**Pay station:** A player who calls bets and raises much more than is correct. He's also referred to as a *calling station.* This type is great when you have a legitimate hand, but he's just about impossible to bluff out of a pot.

**Position:** The spot in the sequence of betting in which a player is located. A player in first position would be the first person to act; a player in last position would be the last person to act.

**Positive expectation:** The amount a wager may be expected to win on average. A play with positive expectation is a play that will win money over the long run.

**Pot:** The total amount of money wagered at any point in a hand. A hand itself is also referred to as a pot. Thus, three people in the pot means there are three active players still playing the hand.

**Pot odds:** The ratio of the amount of money in the pot to the bet you must call to continue in the hand.

**Put someone on a hand:** To determine as best you can the hand (or hands) an opponent is most likely to have.

**Pure nuts:** The best possible hand. If the board is A♥7♦8♦K♠4♠ a player holding a 65 has the pure nuts.

**Rag:** *See* Blank.

**Raise:** To bet an additional amount after someone else has bet.

**Raiser:** A player who raises.

**Rake:** An amount retained by a casino from each pot, usually no more than $2 or $3.

**Represent:** To make your opponents believe you have a better hand than you really do.

**Reraise:** To raise after an opponent has raised.

**Reverse implied odds:** The ratio of the amount of money now in the pot to the amount of money you will have to call to continue from the present round to the end of the hand.

**River:** The fifth and last community card.

**Round of betting:** A sequence of betting after one or more cards have been dealt. A round of betting continues until each active player has either folded or called.

**Royal flush:** An ace-high straight flush. A♠K♠Q♠J♠T♠ is a royal flush.

**Running pair:** Fourth- and fifth-street of the same rank (but of a rank different from any of the other cards on board.)

**Rush:** Several winning hands in a short period of time.

**Sandbag:** To play weakly with a strong hand. To check-raise or slowplay with the probable best hand.

**Score:** A big win.

**Seat charge:** In public card rooms, an hourly fee for playing poker.

**Second pair (third pair):** Pairing the second (third) highest card on board.

**Semi-bluff:** To bet with a hand which you do not think is the best hand but which has a reasonable chance of improving to the best hand.

**Set:** Three-of-a-kind.

**Short odds:** The odds for an event that has a good chance of occurring.

**Short-stacked:** Playing in a game with a relatively small number of chips remaining.

**Showdown:** The turning up of all active players' cards at the end of the final round of betting to see who has the best hand.

**Side pot:** A second pot for the other active players when one player is all-in.

**Slowplay:** To check or just call an opponent's bet with a big hand in order to win more money on later rounds of betting.

**Starting requirement:** The minimum initial hand a player considers he needs to continue in a pot.

**Start the action:** To make the first bet in a particular hand.

**Steal:** To cause your opponents to fold when you probably do not have the best hand. The term is used especially in reference to stealing the antes — that is, raising on the first round of betting so that everyone remaining in the pot folds.

**Steam:** To play badly because you are emotionally upset — especially to play considerably more pots than you normally would when your hands do not justify it.

**Straight:** Five cards of mixed suits in sequence. T♦9♣8♥7♦6♥ is a straight.

**Straight flush:** Five cards of the same suit in sequence. T♥9♥8♥7♥6♥ is a straight flush.

**Structure:** The limits set upon the ante, forced bets, and subsequent bets and raises in any given game.

**Stuck:** Losing money, especially a substantial amount of money, in a given session or over a period of time. We might say, "Sammy is stuck $1,500 in the game." That is, Sammy has lost $1,500.

**Sucker:** A player who can be expected to lose money, especially one who is not as good as he thinks.

**Suited:** Two or more cards of the same suit.

**Tell:** A mannerism a player exhibits that may give away his hand.

**Three-of-a-kind:** Three cards of the same rank. 7♠7♦7♥ is *three-of-a-kind*.

**Tight:** Playing fewer hands than the norm.

**Tight game:** A game with a small number of players in most pots.

**Top pair:** Pairing the highest card on board.

**Trips:** Three-of-a-kind.

**Turn:** The fourth community card. Some "old time" players also refer to the flop as the *turn*.

**Two flush:** Two cards of the same suit.

**Underdog:** A hand that does not have the best chance of winning.

**Under the gun:** The first person to act on the first round of betting is under the gun. On later betting rounds, the player to the immediate left of the bettor is said to be under the gun.

**Up:** Expressions like aces up, kings up, and sixes up mean two pair with two aces, two kings, or two sixes as the highest of the two pair. Unless an opponent has a top pair of the same rank, the rank of the second pair is of no importance.

**Value:** What a hand is worth in terms of its chance of being the best hand.

**Wager:** A bet.

**Wired pair:** A pair in the hole.

**World Series of Poker:** An annual series of poker tournaments with buy-ins ranging up to $10,000, which is held each spring at the Horseshoe Casino in Las Vegas. The competition is generally recognized as the premier competition among the best poker players in the world.

**Worst of it:** A situation in which a wager will be unprofitable in the long run.

# Index